With my
gratitude for making
Sarah's wedding so
beautiful!
Karen Mason

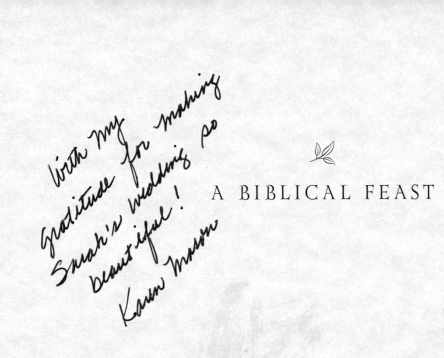

A BIBLICAL FEAST

A BIBLICAL FEAST

Foods from the Holy Land

KITTY MORSE

Photography by
SUSANNE KASPAR

TEN SPEED PRESS
Berkeley, California

A Kirsty Melville Book

1☉ TEN SPEED PRESS
Box 7123, Berkeley, California 94707

Distributed in Australia by Simon & Schuster Australia, in Canada by Publishers Group West, in New Zealand by Tandem Press, in South Africa by Real Books, in Southeast Asia by Berkeley Books, and in the United Kingdom and Europe by Airlift Books.

Cover and text design by Nancy Austin.
Photography by Susanne Kaspar, Berkeley, California.
Food styling and prop assistance by Sue White, San Rafael, California.
Props courtesy of Ethnic Arts, Berkeley, California.

Library of Congress Cataloging-in-Publication Data
Morse, Kitty
A biblical feast : food from the Holy Land / Kitty Morse :
photography by Susanne Kaspar.
p.   cm.
"A Kirsty Melville book"—T.p. verso
Includes index.
ISBN 0-89815-965-2
1. Cookery.   2. Bible—Quotations.   3. Food in the Bible.
I. Title
TX652.M674   1998   98–10102
641.595694—dc21

Printed in Korea

First printing, 1998
1 2 3 4 5 6 7 8 9 10 – 03 02 01 00 99 98

For Owen, with love

*There is nothing better for a man, than that he should eat and drink,
and that he should make his soul enjoy good in his labour…*

ECCLESIASTES 2:24

CONTENTS

He watereth the hills from his chambers:
the earth is satisfied with the fruit of thy works.

He causeth the grass to grow for the cattle,
and herb for the service of man:
that he may bring forth food out of the earth;

And wine that maketh glad the heart of man,
and oil to make his face to shine,
and bread which strengtheneth man's heart.

PSALMS 104:13–15

THE HOLY LAND IN BIBLICAL TIMES

N
W E
S

Sidon

Tyre

Damascus

Sea of Galilee

Nazareth

Jordan River

Qumran

Jerusalem

Dead Sea

Bethlehem

Hebron

Beer Sheva

FROM THE HOLY LAND
TO TODAY'S TABLE

Be not forgetful to entertain strangers
for thereby some have entertained angels unawares.

HEBREWS 13:2

To TRAVEL THROUGH the rural regions of my native Morocco is akin to being transported back to biblical times. There, small farmers work the land in much the same way as their Arab and Berber forebears had centuries earlier: ploughing with camels or oxen and sowing, cultivating, and harvesting by hand. Women and children watch over small flocks of sheep and goats, carry amphorae from nearby wells, or gather firewood to fuel their mud ovens. On market day, farmers clad in traditional *djellabahs* (robes), sandals, and turbans haul their produce to the local *souk* (market) in large, woven straw baskets slung heavily over the backs of submissive donkeys—a biblical tableau come to life.

As a young schoolgirl, I prepared for my confirmation at the quaint Anglican church of Saint John the Evangelist, an island of tranquillity in the heart of downtown Casablanca, Morocco's bustling commercial capital. Somehow, I never considered the obvious similarities between the way of life of the ancient Semitic peoples I was studying in the Bible, and of the people who lived just beyond the city limits.

Years later, while attending an Easter service, I listened to a thought-provoking sermon taken from John 13:20–30. The realization suddenly struck me: Jesus and the disciples had

1

been dining *"à la marocaine"* (Moroccan fashion) or, more accurately, in the popular Greco-Roman style of their day. Leonardo da Vinci created a misconception in his famous wall painting of the Last Supper by portraying the celebrants dining in a spacious, Renaissance-style refectory, seated in chairs along one side of an elegant, linen-covered banquet table. It is far more likely that on that last Passover of His life, Christ gathered with His disciples in the "guest chamber" of a modest dwelling in Jerusalem. After taking part in a ritual hand-washing (customary when eating from a common dish), they took their places on straw mats, rugs, cushions, or divans arranged around an open three-sided square. Here they reclined, casually leaning against one another as they passed a cup of red wine. With fingers as their only utensils, they plucked tender morsels from the communal platter, which was set on a serving table before them. They used chunks of unleavened bread or small bunches of bitter herbs to soak up the savory juices from the dish, as Jesus does when he offers the "sop" to Judas, in keeping with the customary solicitude extended to guests. But what was the dish they shared on that Passover evening? More fundamentally, what constituted the diet of the ancient peoples of Scripture? Intriguing questions.

Naturally, my search for answers began in the Bible. I reviewed the dietary laws in the books of Leviticus (11:1–47) and Deuteronomy (14:3–21), which were intended to set God's chosen people apart from their gentile contemporaries. The laws clearly identified the foods the ancient Hebrews were allowed to eat and those they were to consider "unclean." Among the forbidden foods were pork, rabbit, camel, birds of prey, and any kind of fish that did not have scales (such as catfish, eel, and shellfish), as well as most insects (locusts were the only exception). Some of these forbidden foods, notably pork, were eaten by the Israelites' bitter enemies, the Philistines. This, as well as economic factors, may have contributed to its prohibition. The law also forbade the cooking of kid (goat) in its mother's milk (a Canaanite ritual and, therefore, considered pagan). The gentile population of the Holy Land, and probably a small number of secular Jews, did not follow the Levitical and Deuteronomic dietary code. Jesus and His disciples, however, as religious Jews, must have observed the rules (at least during Christ's lifetime). We can infer this from the disciples' shocked reaction to the news of Peter's encounter and meal with Cornelius and the gentiles

2

in the Mediterranean town of Caesarea (Acts 11:2–3). Popular conceptual attitudes concerning clean and unclean foods were about to change for the followers of Jesus. New Testament passages (Mark 7:15, Acts of the Apostles 11:5–9, Romans 14:20–23, and 1 Corinthians 10:25–26) would effectively nullify the restrictions of Deuteronomy for future generations of Christians.

Peter's supper with the gentiles of Caesarea was more than just the communal partaking of food. The convivial meal confirmed their conversion. Certainly it had long been customary for the Hebrews to seal almost every pact in this manner, whether secular or religious, beginning with Moses and the elders of Israel accepting God's covenant in the Book of Exodus 24:8–11. Breaking bread not only established a sacred covenant between the chosen people and their God, but also between a host and his guests.

Food, drink, and communal meals were so essential to physical life that the authors of Scripture employed them in symbolic ways to convey ideas of spiritual life, growth, and sense of religious community. Food is often used allegorically in the Bible to transmit a spiritual message. The most universally known example is Jesus' offering of bread and wine, symbolizing His body and blood, at the Last Supper.

In the Old Testament, Hebrews demonstrated their obedience to Mosiac law through daily food offerings to God and His priests. The law was quite specific. Two yearling lambs, a tenth of an epah (1 epah equaled $1^1/4$ bushels) of wheat flour, a quarter hin (1 hin equaled 2 gallons) of the purest olive oil, and a quarter hin of wine were needed to fulfill their sacred obligation. Other temple ceremonies and special offerings required rams, firstborn lambs, bulls, doves, and pigeons.

Temple offerings did not mirror the diet of those within the general population, who, for the most part, relied little on meat and poultry for their daily nourishment. They subsisted chiefly on an assortment of fruits, vegetables, and legumes—olives, onions, garlic, leeks, lentils, beans, cucumbers, melons, grapes, pomegranates, figs, dates, and almonds—all of which remain staples of today's eastern Mediterranean cuisines. The rest of their diet was made up of cereal grains like spelt (a primitive variety of wheat), "corn" (wheat), barley, and millet. Often, they simply rubbed off the husks to savor the fresh kernels, or tied nearly ripe ears of grain into small sheaves, which they roasted over an open flame. This is the "parched corn" mentioned in Ruth 2:14. Most of the cereal harvest, however, was dried and crushed under a grindstone to produce meal for gruel or "cakes," and flour for bread. The Bible mentions bread over two hundred and thirty times. For the ancient Hebrews, bread was quite literally the staff of life.

The peoples of Scripture followed a predominantly vegetarian diet for practical rather than philosophical considerations. Most households maintained only a small number of stock animals, some of which were saved for religious offerings. The others were undoubtedly more valuable to their owners as a source of fiber (wool), milk, and milk products. Meat was reserved mainly for special occasions or religious celebrations. The elite, those of the palaces and temples, however, enjoyed meat and fowl on a more regular basis. Goat was the most common meat they consumed, followed by lamb and mutton. Fatted calves, stalled oxen, and fatted fowl (probably geese) were highly prized for their fat content. Unlike modern health-conscious cooks, the ancient Hebrews loved fat and included it in their dishes whenever they had the chance. Although most meat came from domesticated animals, Hebrews from all strata of society supplemented their diets to varying degrees with game like wild goat, gazelle, antelope, roebuck, fallow deer, pigeon, dove, partridge, and quail. Ewes, goats, and kine (cows) provided them with milk and butter, as well as with soured or curdled milk products like cheese and yogurt.

Fish is rarely mentioned in the Old Testament, yet we know it was an important element of the diet. Tyre, an ancient Phoenician port city on the Mediterranean, was famous for its fish (which was probably salted and dried). It is also probable that Tyrians produced a pungent, fermented fish sauce akin to what Romans called *garum* and what the Babylonians called *siqqu;* no doubt a product similar to nuoc mam, the popular Vietnamese condiment. Tyrian merchants exported their fish and fish products to Galilee and south to Jerusalem, where they were sold near the "Fish Gate" mentioned in Nehemiah 13:16 and Zephaniah 1:10.

Fish appears frequently in the New Testament. Of course, Jesus fed the multitudes with loaves and fishes. His first apostles, Peter, Andrew, James, and John, earned their living from

the Sea of Galilee, where they caught everything from sardines and tilapia to large carp. Metaphorically speaking, Jesus promised to make them "fishers of men" (Mark 1:17).

Olives were one of the oldest and most important fruits of the Holy Land. Their cultivation spread from Asia Minor two thousand years before the birth of Christ. The ancient Hebrews crushed the ripe fruit to extract oil, which they used extensively in cooking, adding it in generous quantities to almost every dish to impart moisture, cohesiveness, and flavor. They also must have produced and eaten cured olives, although there is no scriptural proof of this. Olive oil had nonculinary applications as well, serving as a fuel for lamps, an ingredient in medicinal salves, and as a sacred anointment in temple ceremonies.

Grapes grew in even greater abundance than olives. The choicest ones were dried in the sun to produce raisins, but most of the late summer harvest was crushed for its juice, which the ancient Hebrews relished in both its unfermented and fermented states. Grapes and wine were produced for export and for local consumption. They provided a significant source of

5

income, especially during Roman rule. The wine from Bethlehem was of such high quality that it was considered a gift worthy of royalty. Wine was served either hot or cold, and it was always diluted with water. Pomegranates, raisins, dried figs, and dates, although primarily eaten, were also used to make wine.

Although the word "corn" appears over one hundred times in the King James version of the Bible, it is not included in the list of biblical foods that begins on page 11. To seventeenth-century English translators, it did not mean "corn" in the American sense—that is, maize or Indian corn. Their connotation reflected a more general definition, as an edible seed of the predominant cereal plant of a region—and for the Holy Land this meant wheat. Maize, as well as other New World culinary discoveries like tomatoes, potatoes, and sweet peppers and chiles, would not become available to the people of the Old World, including the eastern Mediterranean, until some time in the sixteenth century.

To some, the exclusion of apples (*Malus pumila*) and citrus from the list on pages 11–21 will come as a surprise. Many biblical botanists, however, now believe that the unnamed fruit that Eve gave to Adam in the Garden of Eden was most likely an apricot. Apples were not indigenous to the Holy Land and would not find their way there until well after the death of Christ. The same holds true for virtually all members of the citrus family, with the possible exception of the etrog citron, a large, lemonlike fruit, introduced to the Mediterranean Basin by Alexander the Great in the fourth century B.C. Apricots were eaten fresh, in season, or, like grapes and figs, dried for future consumption.

Salt was the primary seasoning for the people of the Old and New Testaments. They mined it near the infamous city of Sodom, on the edge of the Dead Sea. Biblical cooks also relied on wild and cultivated potherbs like onion, leeks, garlic, dill, lovage, mint, mallow, mustard, coriander (cilantro), and possibly saffron, to flavor their dishes. They gathered wild sesame seeds, which they used primarily, but not exclusively, for their oil. Only the more affluent could afford imported, and therefore relatively expensive, spices like saffron, cassia cinnamon, and black peppercorns (the most popular spice of the ancient world). Sugar was unknown, although the Bible mentions a "sweet cane," (perhaps a variety of wild sugarcane). For sweetening their dishes, biblical cooks relied upon wild honey, honeycomb, or, more frequently, sweet, viscous syrups (called *dibs*) made by boiling down the juice of grapes, pomegranates, figs, and dates. They also used the sap of several species of desert trees that may have been one source of the mysterious manna referred to in Exodus 16:31: "And the house of Israel called the name thereof Manna: and it was like coriander seed, white; and the taste of it was like wafers made with honey."

There has long been controversy among biblical scholars, as to the nature of the food that sustained the Jews in the "wilderness" of the Sinai following their exodus from Egypt. The Bible describes three different kinds of manna, which, according to noted biblical botanists Harold Moldenke, Ph.D., and Alma Moldenke, were composed of a dried form of a species of algae; drought-dessicated and wind-dispersed lichens; and the hardened exudate from insect-perforated stems of certain trees like the tamarisk *(Tamarix mannifera).* To this day, some of the Bedouins in the Holy Land gather and sell this substance, which they call "man." It is an ingredient in traditional Middle Eastern confections.

Biblical cooks prepared their meals in open courtyards outside their homes. They used sticks, dried grasses, and dried cattle dung for fuel. Low boiling (stewing), rather than roasting or frying, was their favorite method of cooking. They baked bread either directly on heated stones, on a griddle, or in small earthen ovens that provided a more humid atmosphere. The Manual of Discipline, one of the Dead Sea Scrolls, provides elaborate details on the dining customs of Qumran, thought to be the City of Salt (Ir-hamelah) of Joshua 15:62, located near the caves where the ancient scrolls were discovered. The site also held more than one thousand cooking utensils, including cauldrons, clay cooking pots, frying pans, pitchers, and even wine vessels made of translucent and clear glass. Except for knives used to butcher and carve meat, and possibly stirring sticks and ladles, the ancient Hebrews prepared and ate most food with their hands.

Although archaeological sites like Qumran provide us with a fascinating assortment of ancient culinary utensils, they give us little insight as to what dishes were prepared with them. Surprisingly, there is almost no mention of cooking techniques in the Bible—not a single recipe, except for a mixed grain and pulse bread in the Book of Ezekiel (Ezekiel 4:9); and this, really, is a list of unquantified ingredients. Fortunately, we have access to the first century A.D.

7

writings of Roman bon vivant and cookbook author Apicius. In addition, Babylonian clay tablets first deciphered in the early 1980s give us a record of the world's oldest existing recipes, dating from two thousand years before Christ. The legacy of this ancient cuisine may have influenced the Hebrews who lived in Mesopotamian exile following the first destruction of the temple in 586 B.C.

Both Apicius and the Babylonian tablets open a window onto their surprisingly advanced cuisine; one prepared primarily by male cooks for the nobility and priestly hierarchy of their respective civilizations. The vast majority of the inhabitants of the ancient Near East, including the Hebrews and early Christians, had neither the financial means to procure expensive and eccentric ingredients, nor the time to assemble elaborate meals. Domestic cooks—women of modest means—were well versed in a more popular form of cookery. They created simple, yet flavorful dishes for their families, or the families they served, using a limited number of readily available ingredients.

It was the wife's duty, or the duty of the female household servant, to bake the family's daily bread and prepare their meals. The ancient Hebrews usually began their day with a light breakfast consisting of milk, a piece of bread, and perhaps butter or cheese. They ate their main meal in the evening (for the poor, this was often the only meal of the day). Supper may have begun with something pickled in brine or vinegar to stimulate the appetite. This was followed by a simple pottage, or a stew of seasonal herbs and garden vegetables, thickened with whole grain or grain meal.

More elaborate dishes, especially those containing meat, were reserved for special celebrations, primarily those of thanksgiving: for release from Egyptian bondage (Passover), deliverance from Babylonian plotters (Purim), or for an abundant harvest, to mention just a few. For this reason, many religious festivals were linked to the seasons, especially to the times of sowing and reaping. Whether the ancient Hebrews were nomadic herdsmen, pastoral nomads, farmers, or fishermen, they regarded the earth's bounty, the food that sustained them, as a gift from God. The celebrations also served as a means of creating and reinforcing the sense of community among God's people. Thus something natural—the sharing of a meal—acquired spiritual significance and bound together people of common faith. And what meal could be simpler than the bread and wine of the Eucharist, derived from the Greek word *eucharistos,* meaning "grateful."

The recipes in this book are based on my study of the Old and New Testaments and related sources, as well as on my knowledge of Mediterranean cuisine. My purpose was not to invent a biblical haute cuisine, but rather to re-create dishes that the ancient inhabitants of the Holy Land might have prepared, always keeping in mind that they were, for the most part, simple people—shepherds, farmers, fishermen, and carpenters—who ate uncomplicated yet wholesome food.

I hope you will use the recipes in this book as the ancient Hebrews and early Christians would have—by gathering around the communal dish to celebrate a religious or secular event or to entertain honored guests. For it is the sharing of food with friends and loved ones that was, and still is, one of life's foremost pleasures.

FOODS OF
THE KING JAMES BIBLE

THIS LIST IS NOT a complete record of every plant and animal that made up the diet of the ancient Hebrews. Many more foodstuffs other than the ones specifically mentioned in the Bible must have been available to them. Understandably, the writers of the Old and New Testaments were far less concerned with botanical, zoological, and culinary matters than they were with those that defined their theology and chronicled prominent figures and events of historical importance to their people.

ALMONDS *(Amygdalus communis):* In the Holy Land, almond blooms heralded the coming of spring. Almond trees were prized for their nuts and for the oil pressed from them and were believed to prevent intoxicating effects of wine. The nuts were commonly mixed with dates or raisins to make confections.

ANISE (more likely, dill, *Anethum graveolens):* A flavoring agent employed in pickling and cooking, anise was also used medicinally as a digestive aid.

APPLES (more likely, apricot, *Prunus armeniaca):* Some noted biblical botanists now believe that the "apple" of Scripture was an apricot or, perhaps, a quince. The apricot better fits the biblical criteria: a pleasant-tasting, fragrant, golden fruit from a shady, silvery-leafed tree.

BARLEY (from genus *Hordeum):* Since prehistoric times, barley has been one of man's primary cereal crops. In biblical times it symbolized poverty, most likely because it was a staple of the poorer classes even though everyone ate it when wheat was scarce. Barley was also used as cattle fodder.

BAY *(Laurus nobilis):* Also called green bay, laurel, or sweet bay. The leaves of the bay tree were an ancient symbol of prosperity. For this reason, laurel wreaths crowned the heads of the great men of Greece and Rome. Bay leaves were also widely used in medicinal preparations and as a flavoring agent in cooking.

BEANS: Known as legumes or pulses (fava beans, *Faba vulgaris,* and garbanzo beans, *Cicer arienitum)*. Favas are the world's most popular beans, despite their relative rarity in the United States. Favas were eaten by the masses throughout the ancient Near East, especially by the poor. They were served alone or combined with other ingredients in vegetable and meat pottages.

BITTER HERBS: The bitter herbs referred to in the Bible may have included arugula (or rocket), chicory, dandelion, endive, lovage, sorrel, and watercress. The herbs were an accompaniment to meat, especially during the Passover feast, where they symbolized the bitterness of Egyptian bondage. Depending upon availability, they were served separately or mixed in salads.

BREAD: Bread was indisputably the staff of life for the ancient Hebrews. The loaves of the Holy Land were made with or without leavening and primarily from wheat, although flours from other cereal grains like barley and spelt were also used exclusively or in combination with wheat flour. Cereal flours could be extended with ground pulse. The inhabitants of the Holy Land used chunks of bread as their only eating utensils.

BULLOCK: A castrated bull, from the species *Bos taurus, Bos indicus,* and possibly *Bubalus bubalis.* Though few in number (in comparison to sheep and goats), they made a substantial contribution to the meat supply because of their size.

BUTTER: Sometimes "butter" refers to soft cheese or cream. Butter was obtained by vigorously churning cream in specially made vessels. The ancients used it for cooking and frying.

CAKES: Small, flattened masses of dough made from grain meal or flour that was cooked by frying or baking. Dried fruit was also compressed into "cakes."

CALF: A young cow or bull, from the species *Bos taurus, Bos Indicus,* and possibly *Bubalus bubalis.* Fatted calves were not ranged-fed, but raised in small enclosures. Their meat was high in fat and therefore greatly valued by the people of the Holy Land.

CAMEL (or dromedary, *Camelus dromedarius):* Prohibited as a source of meat by Leviticus and Deuteronomy. Camel's milk, however, may have been used infrequently, although it was not an important element of the diet. It soured quickly and was considered inferior in flavor to milk from other sources. Camels were pack animals and a source of hair for weaving.

CANE (wild sugarcane, *Saccharum officinarum):* Sugarcane grew wild in the Holy Land. The "sweet cane" of the Bible was chewed as a confection. Techniques for processing sugar were unknown in biblical times.

CHAMOIS: A goatlike antelope hunted as game.

CHEESE: Also called curds, cheese was produced from the milk of goats, ewes, or cows through the action of an enzyme called rennin, or through a process of acidification using acetic acid (vinegar).

CINNAMON *(Cinnamomum zeylanicum):* Important to the ancient Hebrews as a spice, perfume, and additive to sacred annointing oils. Phoenicians imported it into Judea.

COCK: Jesus predicted that Peter would deny him three times before the cock crowed. The fowl he was referring to was probably the chicken *(Gallus domesticus),* which was used for its eggs, meat, and feathers.

CORIANDER *(Coriandrum sativum):* Also called cilantro or Chinese parsley. The seeds and leaves of this plant were used to flavor soups, stews, and, occasionally, wine. They were also used as a digestive aid.

CORN: Biblical translators in the time of King James treated the word "corn" as a generic name for the predominant cereal grain of a region. For the Holy Land, this was wheat (*Triticum aestivum*), not the New World maize. Wheat, or one of its ancient varieties called spelt, has been cultivated in the Near East since the earliest recorded history. It is primarily used to make bread.

CUMIN (*Cuminum cyminum*, or possibly black cumin, *Nigella sativa*): A spice and flavoring agent for meat, stews, and fish, cumin was (and still is) sprinkled over bread.

CUCUMBERS (*Cucumis sativus*): Cultivated in the warmer regions of the Old World since pre-historic times, cucumbers remain widely popular in the Holy Land to this day. In biblical times, a cucumber, a little vinegar, and a piece of bread may have served as a simple meal for members of a poor Hebrew family.

EGGS: Obtained from chickens, geese, quail, and other wild fowl, especially the partridge.

FALLOW DEER (*Dama dama* and *Dama mesopotamica*): One of the game animals that helped supplement the diet of the peoples of the Holy Land.

FATTED FOWL (probably geese): Raised in enclosed areas. Prized for their fat.

FIGS (*Ficus carica*): The fig is the first plant mentioned in Scripture. Next to the grape, it is the most important fruit of the Holy Land. The trees usually produced two crops each year: one in June, called the "first ripe" figs, and another in August and September. The sweet, ripe fruit was eaten out of hand, or dried in the sun. It was pressed into molds to form "cakes" for transporting and storage. Applied as a poultice, figs also had a medical use.

FISH: The ancients ate both freshwater and saltwater fishes. Freshwater fish from the Sea of Galilee included: the Kenneret sardine (*Acanthobrama terrae sanctae*); a species from the carp family (*Cyprinideae*); and tilapia (*Tilapia galilea*), known today as Saint Peter's Fish. Tyrian merchants imported fish caught in the Mediterranean that was preserved in salt, dried, and cured. They also may have produced and imported a fermented fish sauce that the Romans called *garum*.

FITCHES: Most likely refers to spelt or black cumin.

FLOUR: Distinguished from "meal" in that it was ground from only the inner kernels of wheat, called "kidneys of wheat." This was the "finest of wheat," and consequently more expensive.

FOWL: In the case of the ancient Hebrews, edible "fowl" would have included chickens, geese, pigeons, doves, quails, and partridges. "Fatted fowl" was a term that probably referred to geese (genus *Anser)*. Ancient Hebrew carvings depict women carrying geese, which they probably raised in enclosed areas. They were highly valued for their fat.

GARLIC *(Allium sativum):* Cultivated in the eastern Mediterranean at the time of Moses. Like other members of the *Allium* family (onions and leeks), garlic was extremely popular. It was eaten raw with bread, used in cooking to flavor food, and was considered a digestive stimulant, diuretic, and antispasmodic.

GOAT *(Capra hircus):* Goats represented a village or household resource. They were primarily valued for their milk and meat, which was, however, considered inferior to lamb or mutton. Goat meat was the cheapest type available to the ancient Hebrews. Goats were hardier and more drought tolerant than sheep. They were able to inhabit mountainous terrain.

GOURDS: The gourds referenced in the Bible were probably opo squashes, *Lagenaria leucantha*, which originated in Abyssinia. Still popular in the Mediterranean today, they grow 2 to 3 feet in length and are characterized by a long crooked neck and a pale green, slightly fuzzy skin.

GRAPES *(Vitus vinifera):* Symbolic of both the Jewish nation and later the Christian Church. Grapes are the first cultivated plant mentioned in the Bible. The vineyards of the Holy Land were renowned for the enormous clusters of grapes they produced. The grapes were eaten fresh or dried into raisins and compressed into "cakes." Their juice was drunk unfermented as "new wine," or in its fermented state. Through boiling, the unfermented grape juice produced a syrupy sweet condiment called dibs or grape honey. The Hebrews exported it to Tyre.

HART: An adult male deer that was hunted by the ancient Hebrews.

HEN: Principally, chickens *(Gallus domesticus),* which were used for their eggs, meat, and feathers.

HONEY: The ancient Hebrews obtained honey, their main sweetening agent, from hives found in the hollows of trees and rocks. The word "honey," however, is believed to have had a more generic definition, one that included not only bee honey, but also the sweet syrups (called dibs) that were made from dates, grapes, and pomegranates. Honey symbolized wealth. (No wonder the Promised Land was described as the "the land of milk and honey.")

HONEYCOMB: The wax structure made by bees to store their honey.

HUSKS: Probably refers to pods from the carob tree *(Ceratonia siliqua),* which were only eaten in times of famine, or on a regular basis by the desperately poor. They were also a source of cattle fodder. According to some biblical scholars, John the Baptist lived on a diet of carobs and honey, not locusts and honey. They believe the mistranscription of a single letter, changed the Hebrew word for "carob" into "locust." Today, carob is often used as a chocolate substitute.

HYSSOP: Most likely, the word "hyssop" referred to the caper bush *(Capparis sicula).* Young caper buds were pickled in vinegar and used as a condiment for meat and fish.

JUNIPER ROOT: This was most likely a parasitic plant *(Cynamorium coccineum)* that was common around the Dead Sea. It was eaten only in times of severe food shortages and was used to treat intestinal ailments.

KID: A young goat *(Capra hircus).* See GOAT.

KINE: Cows, from the species *Bos taurus, Bos indicus,* and possibly *Bubalus bubalis.*

LAMB: A young sheep. Lambs were slaughtered to honor a guest or mark a special religious or secular event.

LEAVEN: A small piece of the previous day's yeast-fermented dough, which was mixed with water in the first step of bread making. The ancient Hebrews were prohibited from preparing leavened bread for sacred occasions because leaven was thought to corrupt the natural dough.

LEEKS *(Allium porum):* Leeks grew wild, but were also cultivated in the Holy Land. Although they were a favorite of the ancient Egyptians and Hebrews, they were considered a food of the poor and consequently became a symbol of humility. Leeks were typically prepared in vinegar, cooked in pottages or eaten raw with bread.

LENTILS *(Lens esculenta):* Several varieties of lentils were cultivated in the ancient Near East. Red lentils (actually yellow-brown in color) were the most frequently grown variety and the ones most likely used to prepare the pottage for which Esau relinquished his right of primogeniture. Lentil meal was also used in bread making.

LIQUOR: Also referred to as "strong drink" in the Bible. Probably made from a syrupy liquid obtained from the date palm.

LOCUST *(Aedipodia migratoria* or *Acrydium peregrinum):* Locusts were the only insect the ancient Hebrews were allowed to eat, under provisions set forth in the Old Testament. The locusts' redeeming characteristic was having "legs above their feet, to leep withal upon the earth" (Leviticus 11:21). They were roasted and eaten in the ancient Near East, and may have constituted part of the diet of John the Baptist, although there is some debate about this (see HUSKS).

MALLOW: Probably sea purslane *(Atriplex halimus).* Related to spinach and abundant in and around the Dead Sea.

MANNA: The miraculous "dew from heaven" of Exodus. The Bible mentions three distinct kinds of manna, which, according to a prominent biblical botanist, was composed of (1) a dried form of algae; (2) dessicated, wind-dispersed lichens; and (3) the hardened exudate from the insect-perforated stems of certain desert trees like the *Tamarix mannifera.*

17

MEAL: Made from ground whole cereal grains and bran, meal was considered inferior to flour and therefore relatively inexpensive. It was used in gruel and to thicken pottage.

MILK (from sheep, goats, and cows): Fresh milk as well as its derivatives—cream, yogurt, cheese, and butter—formed an important part of the diet in the "land of milk and honey." The ancient Hebrews preferred goat's milk to ewe's milk, and either of these to the milk of cows (kine). Milk was drunk fresh or kept for short periods in "bottles" made from skins.

MILLET *(Panicum miliaceum):* The smallest grained cereal grass cultivated by man. Perhaps the least popular of the biblical cereals, it was eaten by the poor.

MINT (probably horse mint, *Mentha longifolia):* An aromatic plant known throughout the ancient Near East as a flavoring agent, condiment, and digestive aid.

MELONS (probably muskmelon, *Cucumis melo,* and watermelon, *Citrullus vulgaris):* Both muskmelons and watermelons were recorded early in history as having been cultivated in Egypt. They were widely popular there and in the Holy Land as a source of food and drink. The juice of the overripe watermelon had medicinal value as well; it was used to treat fevers.

MULBERRY (black or red, *Morus nigra):* The mulberry mentioned in 2 Samuel 23 is believed to be the black mulberry.

MUSTARD SEED *(Brassica negra):* Described as "the least of all seeds" in the parable of Matthew 13:31–32, mustard seed was ground for its oil and used as a condiment.

NUTS: The "nuts" mentioned in the Bible were probably pistachios (*Pistacia vera*), and walnuts (*Juglans regia*). They were included in the gift of food that Jacob sent to Egypt. Pistachios have been widely cultivated since the time of Solomon, and are used both in cooking and confectionery. Roman historian Josephus writes of their abundance in Palestine, particularly in the region around the Sea of Galilee.

OLIVES *(Olea europaea):* Olives are the fruit most closely associated with civilization. They were of incalculable economic and nutritional value to the ancient Hebrews. The olive branch was, and is, a symbol of peace and prosperity.

OLIVE OIL: Olive oil was extracted from the fruit by crushing it with a heavy stone wheel. It is a tremendously versatile product. Biblical cooks added it to almost every dish they prepared. The ancient Hebrews also used it in temple offerings, in sacred anointments, as fuel in their lamps, and as a dressing for wounds.

ONIONS *(Allium cepa):* Onions have been cultivated in Egypt since the earliest times, and were an essential element in the diet of the poor. The wealthy added generous amounts of onions to meat and vegetable dishes.

OX: Any of the several species of bovid animals, domesticated or wild, from the genus *Bos.* Stalled oxen, those raised in enclosed areas, were prized for the high-fat content of their meat.

PALMS (date palms, *Phoenix dactylifera):* Date palms have been used as a model for architectural ornamentations since the time of Solomon's temple. Greek historian Herodotus (5 B.C.) writes of the products obtained from the tree: "Bread" (raw dates), wine, and honey (dibs). Biblical scholars believe that at one time the Jordan River Valley was almost entirely covered with date palms. This explains why Jericho, a city at the southern end of the valley, was known as "the city of palms" and why the palm tree symbolized Palestine.

PARTRIDGE *(Cacabis chukar* or *Ammoperdix heyi):* A game bird hunted for its meat and eggs.

PIGEON *(Colomba livia):* With turtledoves, the most commonly eaten fowl in the Holy Land. Also used in temple offerings.

POMEGRANATES *(Punica granatum):* These ornamental-looking fruits were symbolic of fertility and considered one of the "pleasant fruits of Egypt." The seeds were eaten out of hand or crushed for their juice, which was boiled down to produce a syrupy, sweet-sour condiment called dibs or pomegranate honey (today it is marketed as pomegranate molasses). Pomegranate juice was also fermented into wine. In addition, pomegranate juice was believed to have antiseptic properties.

PULSE: Edible seeds of pod-bearing plants, such as lentils, fava beans, and garbanzo beans.

PYGARG: Probably a species of antelope or gazelle, hunted by the ancient Hebrews.

QUAIL *(Coturnix communis):* Quail were among the game hunted by the ancient Hebrews. The birds were bountiful in the desert regions of the Holy Land during their annual migration.

RAISINS *(Vitis vinifera):* Produced by sun-drying the choicest grapes of the harvest.

RIE: This was probably *Triticum aestivum,* var. *spelta,* and not rye as we know it. Also called "fitches" and "spelt," rie was a hardy and ancient variety of wheat.

ROEBUCK (male of the roe deer): A game animal hunted by the ancient Hebrews.

RUE *(Ruta chalepensis* or possibly *Ruta graveolens):* An herb used as a seasoning that was also believed to have antiseptic qualities.

SALT: The most common seasoning in biblical times, salt was produced by evaporation from sea water or mined near the infamous city of Sodom. Salt was important symbolically to the ancient Hebrews, whether for establishing a covenant between host and guest, or for signifying the absolute destruction of a city.

SAFFRON *(Crocus sativus):* Prized for its sweet scent, saffron was used to perfume public places or to enhance the flavor of wine. In biblical times, it was used medicinally as a stimulant and antispasmodic. Today, saffron is the world's most expensive spice.

SHEEP *(Ovis saries):* Sheep were the first pastoral animals domesticated and were valued for their wool as well as for their meat. The sheep of the Holy Land were of the fat-tailed variety, according to Greek historian Herodotus, who lived in the fifth century B.C.

SPARROW (from the genus *Passer):* In biblical times, two sparrows were "sold for a farthing" (one-quarter of an English penny), according to Matthew 10:29. They were infrequently eaten, and were the poor's substitute for goat or lamb in temple sacrifices.

SPELT (probably *Triticum aestivum,* var. *spelta):* A primitive variety of wheat also called "rie" in the King James Bible. See also RIE.

SYCOMORE-FIG (*Ficus sycomorus):* Smaller than the common fig, and of inferior quality.

TURTLEDOVES *(Stretopelia turtur):* Like pigeon, this migratory bird was one of the most commonly eaten fowl in the Holy Land. It probably was not domesticated and was frequently used in temple offerings.

VINEGAR: Simply defined, vinegar is soured wine. It is made from wine or other alcoholic beverages which are inoculated with certain bacteria, causing fermentation and the formation of acetic acid (vinegar). In biblical times, vinegar diluted with water was a refreshing drink for laborers working in the harvest fields. Of course, it was also employed as a condiment in cookery and as a pickling agent.

WHEAT: See CORN.

WINE: The wine of the Holy Land was classified as either "new wine" (unfermented) or "old wine" (fermented). Wine was produced primarily from grapes *(Vitis vinifera),* although pomegranates, raisins, dried figs, and dates were also used. Grape wine was considered superior to the others and "old wine" was valued more highly than "new wine."

SIMPLE DISHES

Ground Sesame Seed Dip

Leek Dip

Toasted Ground Almond and Sesame Dip

Cumin-Laced Garbanzo Bean Spread

Flatbread and Goat Cheese with Melon

Brine-Cured Seasoned Olives

Bitter Herb Salad

Lentil Salad with Watercress and Goat Cheese

Millet with Saffron and Walnuts

Fresh Fava Beans with Olive Oil and Garlic

Braised Cucumbers and Leeks with Fresh Dill

Fried Fava Beans

Dilled Cucumbers with Olives and Goat Cheese

Leeks with Olive Oil, Vinegar, and Mustard Seed

Squash with Capers and Mint

Ground Sesame Seed Dip

Sesame seeds were an important crop for the peoples of the ancient Near East because of the high quality of the oil and meal they provided. Archaeologists have found evidence of sesame cultivation in Egypt, Palestine, Babylonia, and Assyria. North of the Assyrian capital, Nineveh, they discovered crushed seeds in their excavations of the kingdom of Ararat (Jeremiah 51:27). In ancient times, sesame oil was primarily employed as a fuel for lamps. However, it had culinary, medicinal, and cosmetic applications as well.

Although sesame seeds are not specifically mentioned in the Bible, the ancient Hebrews certainly must have used them in their cooking. To this day, they are a ubiquitous ingredient in the cuisines of the eastern Mediterranean. When lightly toasted and ground into a paste, sesame seeds add a nutty flavor to a wide variety of sauces, dips, and dressings (see Note).

$1/2$ cup hulled sesame seeds

$1/4$ cup water

$1/2$ teaspoons white wine vinegar

$1/4$ teaspoon salt

1 small clove garlic, minced

Olive oil

Bitter herbs (such as arugula, chicory, dandelion, endive, sorrel, or watercress), washed and dried, or Unleavened Griddle Bread (see page 74)

Toast the sesame seeds $1/4$ cup at a time, following the instructions on page 107. Immediately after the seeds are toasted, grind them into a paste using a mortar and pestle, electric spice grinder, or grain mill. Transfer the paste to a small serving bowl, and mix with the water. Stir in the vinegar, salt, and garlic, and mix well. Drizzle with olive oil. Serve at room temperature with the bitter herbs or bread for dipping.

Note: Commercially prepared sesame butter, marketed as tahini, is available in health food stores, and gourmet and Middle Eastern markets.

Makes about $1/2$ cup

Leek Dip

We remember the fish, which we did eat in Egypt freely;
the cucumbers, and the melons, and the leeks,
and the onions, and the garlic…

NUMBERS 11:5

Although the original Hebrew word for leek in Numbers 11:5 was literally translated as "green herb," most biblical scholars concur that the writers of the Old Testament must have meant "leek" since it was linked with onions and garlic, also members of the *Allium* family. The ancient Hebrews were particularly fond of these three vegetables. They ate leeks raw with vinegar and bread or cooked them in broth or oil. Leeks are still as popular in the Near East today as they were in biblical times. For this recipe, cook the leeks to a spreadlike consistency in order to fully enjoy their mild, sweet flavor. I use this as a dip for raw vegetables or as a spread for wedges of warm Leavened Griddle Bread (see page 76) or Unleavened Griddle Bread (see page 74).

2 leeks

2 tablespoons olive oil

Salt to taste

Trim and thoroughly rinse the leeks under running water. Finely chop the white bulblike ends and tender green parts of the stem.

Heat the olive oil in a skillet over medium heat. Add the leeks and cook until they are lightly caramelized, 15 to 20 minutes. Transfer to a serving bowl and lightly mash with a fork. Season with salt and serve.

Makes about 1/2 cup

Toasted Ground Almond and Sesame Dip

Variations of this delicious blend of ground nuts and spices are popular throughout the Near East, and it is not unlikely that the ancient Hebrews were familiar with one like it. Traditionally, a piece of bread is first dipped into olive oil, and then into the dry dip.

½ cup whole blanched almonds, toasted (see page 107)

½ teaspoon whole cumin seed, toasted (see page 107)

2 tablespoons unhulled sesame seeds, toasted (see page 109)

2 teaspoons nigella seeds (see Note)

¼ teaspoon salt

In a spice grinder, grain mill, or stone grinding implement (such as a Mexican *molcajete*), grind the almonds to the consistency of coarse bread crumbs. Transfer them to a bowl. Coarsely grind the cumin seeds and add them to the almonds. Stir in the sesame seeds, nigella seeds, and salt.

To serve, place a small bowl of extra virgin olive oil in the center of the table, alongside a bowl of the almond mixture. To eat, dip a piece of bread in the oil, then in the almonds.

Note: *Nigella sativa,* the seed of the nutmeg flower (not related to true nutmeg), sometimes called black cumin, is an annual plant of the buttercup family that produces tiny black seeds with a distinct, peppery taste. It grows wild around the Mediterranean. Pliny, a Roman naturalist who lived between 23 B.C. and A.D. 79, comments in his writings on the frequent use of black cumin as a flavoring for bread. For a source for nigella, see page 108.

Makes 1 cup

26

*And it came to pass, that on the morrow Moses went
into the tabernacle of witness; and, behold, the rod of Aaron
for the house of Levi was budded, and brought forth buds,
and bloomed blossoms, and yielded almonds.*

NUMBERS 17:8

Cumin-Laced Garbanzo Bean Spread

For the fitches are not threshed with a threshing instrument,
neither is a cart wheel turned about upon the cummin; but the fitches
are beaten out with a staff, and the cummin with a rod.

ISAIAH 28:27

Garbanzo beans, like fava beans and lentils, are all members of the pulse family. They are among the oldest foods known to humankind. In western Turkey, archaeobontanists have discovered remains of garbanzo beans that date back to 5,500 B.C.

Cumin was a highly prized spice in biblical times. The annual plant is native to the eastern Mediterranean, and remains widely cultivated there today. Some farmers still thresh the seeds "with a rod," using the age-old method described in the Book of Isaiah. Whole cumin seeds were sprinkled on breads and cakes. Ground cumin added its distinctive flavor to stews and simple dishes like this garbanzo bean spread.

1 cup dried garbanzo beans

4 garlic cloves, minced

3/4 teaspoon salt

2 teaspoons white wine vinegar

2 teaspoons cumin seeds, toasted
    and ground (see pages 105, 107)

2 tablespoons olive oil

Unleavened Griddle Bread
    (see page 74), cut into wedges

1 cucumber, peeled and thinly
    sliced

Soak and cook the garbanzo beans, following the directions on page 106. Drain, reserving 3/4 cup of the cooking liquid.

In a food mill or a blender, combine the beans, cooking liquid, garlic, salt, vinegar, and cumin. Process until smooth. Add the olive oil, and mix thoroughly. Transfer the spread to a small bowl. Spread each wedge of bread with the garbanzo mixture, top with cucumber slices, and serve.

Makes 2 cups

Flatbread and Goat Cheese with Melon

And honey, and butter, and sheep, and cheese of kine, for David, and for
the people that were with him, to eat: for they said,
The people is hungry, and weary, and thirsty, in the wilderness.

2 SAMUEL 17:29

There is still some doubt whether the melon mentioned in the Bible refers to muskmelon or watermelon. Both have been cultivated extensively in ancient Egypt for thousands of years. In this recipe, a sweet chunk of ripe melon offers the perfect counterbalance to each bite of bread and goat cheese. This refreshing summer dish is popular in many parts of the Near East.

4 slices muskmelon, peeled, seeded,
  and cubed

4 slices watermelon, peeled, seeded,
  and cubed

Unleaved Griddle Bread (see page 74)
  or Leavened Griddle Bread
  (see page 76)

4 ounces goat cheese, crumbled

In the center of a shallow serving platter, arrange the muskmelon and watermelon cubes. Surround with wedges of bread topped with goat cheese, and serve.

Serves 4

Brine-Cured Seasoned Olives

The trees went forth on a time to anoint a king over them;
and they said unto the olive tree, Reign thou over us.

JUDGES 9:8

What would the Mediterranean landscape be like today without the olive? The venerable trees with their gray-green leaves were likely just as plentiful in the biblical era, judging by the number of times (fifty-five) the word "olive" appears in the Bible. Even in biblical times, the Jordan River Valley and the towns of Lachish and Beth-shemesh were famous for their olives. Many of the cylindrical stone presses used to extract the fruit's flavorful oil are still on display in Israel today.

The ancient Hebrews must have eaten cured olives, even though this is not expressly stated in the Bible. We know that the Romans, who conquered Palestine in 63 B.C., employed lye (an alkaline solution obtained by the leeching of wood ashes) to remove the bitter flavor from raw olives. In this recipe, we cure them with brine.

Sea salt or kosher salt

Water

1 egg, washed

2 pounds firm, unblemished purple
  or black olives, stemmed

Red wine

Red wine vinegar

2 tablespoons olive oil

2 to 3 dill sprigs, finely minced

Minced garlic to taste

Prepare the brine by adding 1 tablespoon of salt to 1 quart of cold water. Use the egg to test the salinity of the solution. When the egg floats to the surface, exposing an area of shell 2.5 centimeters in diameter, the salinity is perfect. Continue adding 1 tablespoon salt and 1 quart of water, retesting with the egg each time, until the right salinity is achieved.

Place the olives and the brine in a glazed, earthenware crock. Use a plate, smaller than the diameter of the crock, to keep the olives submerged below the surface of the brine. Cover the crock with a lid and set it aside in a cool place, for 3 months. Stir the olives once a week. After three months, remove an olive with a slotted spoon. It should be slightly firm to the touch. (In the unlikely event that the olive is soft and/or has a rancid or foul odor, discard it and the remaining olives immediately.) Taste the olive. Most of the bitterness should have disappeared. The color of some olives fades during curing, so don't be concerned if the olives are irregular in color. When submerged in the brine solution and unrefrigerated, the olives keep for up to one year.

With a slotted spoon, transfer the olives you plan to use from the brine to a colander, and rinse well under cold water. Alternatively, soak the cured olives in cold water overnight to reduce excess saltiness. Drain.

Place the olives in a jar or bowl, and add 1 part red wine and 1 part red wine vinegar. Top with a thin layer of olive oil, which acts as a natural seal. Using a slotted spoon, transfer the olives to a serving bowl and mix in the dill and garlic. Serve at room temperature. Refrigerate any uneaten seasoned olives.

Makes 2 pounds

His branches shall spread, and his beauty shall be
as the olive tree, and his smell as Lebanon.
HOSEA 14:6

Bitter Herb Salad

The fourteenth day of the second month at even they shall keep it,
and eat it with unleavened bread and bitter herbs.

NUMBERS 9:11

The bitter herbs served with the paschal lamb on the feast of Passover are meant to symbolize the hardships suffered by the ancient Hebrews during their bondage in Egypt. The exact nature of the herbs, however, remains the subject of debate. Since most were gathered in the wild, they may have varied slightly from one area to another. According to some botanists, common chicory, lettuce, arugula, watercress, mallow, purslane, dandelion, mint, lovage, and sorrel are the most likely candidates.

The word "salad" is derived from the Latin word *salata*, meaning "salted," so named, perhaps, for the way in which greens like bitter herbs were first eaten—simply dipped into salted water—especially during the Passover meal, when salted water symbolized the tears of the Israelites held in Egyptian bondage. The ancient Hebrews probably ate bitter herbs this way. They also flavored the herbs with the savory juices from a communal dish, or with a mixture of wine vinegar and olive oil, like the one in this recipe.

DRESSING

¹/₂ cup extra virgin olive oil

2 tablespoons wine vinegar

2 garlic cloves, minced

¹/₂ teaspoon salt

¹/₄ teaspoon mustard seeds, toasted and
   ground (see pages 105, 107)

SALAD

10 fresh mint leaves

4 cups mixed greens (including bitter
   herbs/greens, such as chicory,
   arugula, watercress, mallow,
   purslane, dandelion greens, lovage,
   and sorrel), washed, dried, and
   torn into bite-sized pieces

10 dry-cured black olives (optional)

To make the dressing, whisk together the oil, vinegar, garlic, salt, and ground mustard in a small bowl. Set aside.

In a salad bowl, toss the mint leaves and mixed greens with the dressing.

Garnish with olives, and serve.

Serves 4

Lentil Salad with Watercress and Goat Cheese

Prove thy servants, I beseech thee, ten days;
and let them give us pulse to eat, and water to drink.

DANIEL 1:12

Lentils originated in the Near East over 9,000 years ago, one of the first pulses (edible seeds from pod-bearing plants) to be cultivated. This protein- and carbohydrate-rich food was highly favored by the ancient Egyptians, who considered the diminutive pulse an aphrodisiac. Frescoes depicting the preparation of lentil pottage date back to the time of the pharaoh Ramses II. Lentils became a popular staple of the biblical diet as well. Dried lentils were ground into meal, then blended with wheat or spelt flour to make bread, or they were served in stews (such as the one on page 50), or in nourishing salads like this one.

…give me thy vineyard, that I may have it for a garden of herbs
because it is near unto my house…

1 KINGS 21:2

DRESSING

1 tablespoon red wine vinegar

1 tablespoon water

3 tablespoons olive oil

1 clove garlic, minced

$1/2$ teaspoon mustard seeds,
   toasted and ground
   (see page 105, 107)

$1/2$ teaspoon salt

SALAD

$3/4$ cup lentils, cooked and drained
   (see page 105)

1 green onion, very finely
   chopped

20 sprigs watercress, leaves only

1 ounce goat cheese, crumbled

4 quail eggs, boiled, shelled, and
   halved (optional)

To prepare the dressing, blend together the vinegar, water, olive oil, garlic, mustard, and salt in a small bowl. Set aside.

To prepare the salad, combine the lentils, green onion, and watercress in a serving bowl. Add the dressing and toss well to coat evenly.

Sprinkle the goat cheese over the salad. Garnish with the quail eggs, and serve immediately.

Serves 4

Millet with Saffron and Walnuts

Thy plants are an orchard of pomegranates, with pleasant fruits; camphire,
with spikenard, Spikenard and saffron; calamus and cinnamon, with all
trees of frankincense; myrrh and aloes, with all the chief spices…

SONG OF SOLOMON 4:13–14

Ancient Phoenicians made dye from the saffron flower (*Crocus sativus*), Egyptians anointed their pharaohs with its oil, and wealthy Romans, believing in its purported aphrodisiacal power, scattered its precious stigmas on the floors of their homes. The aromatic saffron filaments have added color and flavor to dishes since the time of King Solomon. Today it is the world's most expensive spice.

In this recipe, crunchy walnuts complement the pleasant, nutty flavor of millet seeds, one of the oft-mentioned "fitches" in the Bible.

1 cup millet

2 1/2 cups (20 ounces) lamb or
  beef stock (see page 48) or
  commercial broth

6 threads saffron, crushed

4 sprigs cilantro (coriander leaves)

4 green onions or small leeks
  (green parts only), finely
  chopped

1/2 cup walnut pieces, toasted
  (see page 107)

1/2 cup plain yogurt (optional)

In a large skillet over high heat, toast the millet until it begins to pop, 1 to 2 minutes. Transfer the millet to a medium saucepan. Add the stock and the saffron, cover, and bring to a boil. Decrease the heat to medium, and cook until the liquid is absorbed, 35 to 40 minutes. Remove from the heat and fluff with a fork.

In a medium bowl, combine the millet, cilantro, green onions, and walnuts. Serve with a dollop of yogurt on the side.

Serves 4

Fresh Fava Beans with Olive Oil and Garlic

A land of wheat, and barley, and vines, and fig trees,
and pomegranates; a land of oil olive, and honey...

DEUTERONOMY 8:8

Charred remains of fava beans, dating back to 4500 B.C., have been unearthed at Yiftah'el, near Nazareth. They are as extensively cultivated in the eastern Mediterranean today as they were in biblical times. The ancient Hebrews probably ate the beans raw, dipped in a little salt, which is still a popular way of serving them today. Most likely, biblical cooks also boiled the beans and flavored them with olive oil and garlic, as in this recipe. (Before you prepare fava beans, see the warning about favism on page 106.)

1/2 cup water

2 pounds fresh fava beans, shelled
(about 1 cup)

1/4 cup olive oil

3 green onions

3 garlic cloves, minced

1 teaspoon red wine vinegar

1/2 teaspoon cumin seeds, toasted
and ground (see page 105, 107)

Salt to taste

In a small saucepan over medium-high heat, combine the water, fava beans, and 1 tablespoon of the olive oil. Cook, covered, until the beans are tender, 20 to 25 minutes.

Meanwhile, trim the onions and cut them into 1/4-inch-long slices.

Drain the fava beans, transfer them to a serving bowl, and toss with the green onions. In a small bowl, combine the remaining 3 tablespoons of the olive oil, the garlic, vinegar, and cumin. Stir to mix well, then season with salt. Pour the dressing over the beans, and mix well to coat evenly. Serve at room temperature.

Serves 4

37

Braised Cucumbers and Leeks with Fresh Dill

Biblical scholars believe that the herb referred to as "anise" in Matthew 23:23 of the King James Bible was more likely to have been wild dill than the licorice-flavored spice we cook with today. This theory was legitimized when "anise" was changed to "dill" in a recent edition of the New American Bible. Serve this the way the ancients would have: as an accompaniment to roasted meats.

The ancient Hebrews consumed great quantities of cucumbers and leeks during their 400-year enslavement in Egypt. The Romans, who under General Pompey conquered Palestine in 63 B.C., were also great aficionados of the two vegetables. They ate leeks and cucumbers raw with bread, marinated in vinegar, or cooked in an herb-flavored broth.

Woe unto you, scribes and Pharisees, hypocrites! for ye pay tithe
of mint and anise and cummin, and have omitted the weightier matters
of the law, judgment, mercy, and faith: these ought ye to have done,
and not to leave the other undone.

MATTHEW 23:23

3 leeks

1 tablespoon butter

1 tablespoon olive oil

1 large cucumber, peeled, seeded, and cut into 3-inch-long, $1/2$-inch-wide strips (see Note)

2 tablespoons minced fresh dill

1 teaspoon salt

To clean the leeks, remove the tough outer leaves until only the pale yellowish ones remain. Trim the tops. Cut the trimmed leeks crosswise into $1/2$-inch slices. Transfer to a colander, and rinse thoroughly under running water. Drain.

In a heavy skillet over medium heat, melt the butter and heat the olive oil. Add the leeks and cook, stirring occasionally, until golden brown, 8 to 10 minutes. Add the cucumber and dill. Cover and cook until the cucumbers are tender, 10 to 15 minutes. Remove from the heat, season with salt, and serve.

Note: Seedless hothouse cucumbers are best for braising.

Serves 4

Fried Fava Beans

…and Barzillai the Gileadite of Rogelin,
Brought beds and basons, and earthen vessels, and wheat,
and barley, and flour, and parched corn, and beans,
and lentils, and parched pulse.

2 SAMUEL 17:27–28

Fava beans, also called broad beans or horse beans, belong to the pulse family. They are not well known in the United States, although they rank as the world's most widely consumed beans. The ancient peoples of the Holy Land must have looked forward to the harvest of delicious, fresh fava beans each spring. They often dried the beans, or ground them with other pulses and grains to make bread. It is interesting to note that both the French and Italian words for bread (*pain* and *pane,* respectively) are derived from the Greek word for fava bean (*puanos*). In parts of today's Near East, tender young beans are sometimes eaten raw, simply dipped in salt. They are also boiled, tossed with olive oil, and flavored with fresh herbs to make salads. Dried fava beans are soaked in water, then fried in oil and seasoned with salt and spices for a savory snack. They are an essential ingredient in a number of nourishing Middle Eastern soups. (Before you prepare fava beans, see the warning about favism on page 106.)

1 cup dried, peeled, and halved
    fava beans (see Note)

1 cup vegetable or olive oil, or
    more as needed

1 teaspoon salt

1 teaspoon cumin seeds, toasted
    and ground (see page 105, 107)

Place the fava beans in a large bowl, and cover them with 4 inches of water. Soak for 12 to 24 hours. Drain the beans and pat dry.

In a large saucepan over medium-high heat, heat 1 cup of oil until a fava bean sizzles when dropped in the oil. Deep-fry the fava beans a few at a time until they turn golden brown and float to the surface. With a slotted spoon, transfer the beans to a plate lined with paper towels and let them drain. Repeat until all of the beans have been fried and drained.

Place the beans in a serving bowl, sprinkle with the salt and cumin, and serve at room temperature. The beans will keep for up to 1 week in an airtight container at room temperature.

Note: Dried fava beans are available in Middle Eastern and natural foods markets.

Makes about 2 cups

Dilled Cucumbers with Olives and Goat Cheese

And the daughter of Zion is left as a cottage in a vineyard,
as a lodge in a garden of cucumbers, as a besieged city.

ISAIAH 1:8

The "lodge" in Isaiah 1:8 offered shelter to a watchman whose job it was to guard a precious crop of cucumbers. The succulent green fruit is still widely popular in the Middle East, especially in salads mixed with ingredients like yogurt, feta cheese, garlic, mint, olives, and tomatoes, to name just a few. I prefer to use seedless hothouse cucumbers in this refreshing salad, and I serve it with Unleavened Griddle Bread (see page 74) or Leavened Griddle Bread (see page 76).

1 cucumber

12 kalamata olives, pitted and coarsely chopped

1 tablespoon red wine vinegar

2 sprigs fresh dill, finely chopped

4 ounces goat cheese, crumbled

Peel and seed the cucumber. Cut it lengthwise into $1/2$-inch-wide sticks, then crosswise into $1/2$-inch cubes. Place in a serving bowl and set aside.

Gently mix the cucumbers with the olives, vinegar, and dill. Sprinkle with goat cheese.

Serves 4 to 6

Leeks with Olive Oil, Vinegar, and Mustard Seed

*It is like a grain of mustard seed, which a man took,
and cast into his garden; and it grew, and waxed a great tree;
and the fowls of the air lodged in the branches of it.*

LUKE 13:19

The ancient Hebrews, Egyptians, and Romans, were all particularly fond of leeks, a mild-flavored relative of the onion. Apicius, an author and eccentric bon vivant who lived around the time of Christ, lists a number of recipes for leeks in his cookbook, *Apicius de re Coquinaria*. The slender, scallionlike vegetables, available at farmers' markets in early spring, are probably closest to those of biblical times. I like to serve this salad with Unleavened Griddle Bread (see page 74).

3 large leeks

1 tablespoon red wine vinegar

1¼ teaspoons mustard seeds, toasted (see page 107)

2 tablespoons olive oil

Salt and pepper to taste

Thoroughly rinse the leeks under running water. Trim and cut them crosswise into ½-inch-thick slices. Bring a stockpot of water to a boil, add the leeks, and cook until very soft, 20 to 25 minutes. Drain, then place them in a serving dish and set aside.

Using a mortar and pestle or an electric spice grinder, finely grind 1 teaspoon of the toasted mustard seeds. In a small bowl, blend the vinegar and the ground mustard. Slowly whisk in the olive oil. Season with salt and pepper. Spoon this mixture over the leeks. Sprinkle with the remaining ¼ teaspoon whole mustard seeds, and serve at room temperature.

Serves 4

43

Squash with Capers and Mint

And the Lord God prepared a gourd, and made it to come up over Jonah,
that it might be a shadow over his head, to deliver him from his grief.
So Jonah was exceeding glad of the gourd.

JONAH 4:6

Biblical botanists are uncertain as to the exact species of "gourd" or squash referred to in Jonah 4:6. The most likely candidate is a white-flowered gourd whose Latin name is *Lagenaria leucantha*. It is related to a squash native to Abyssinia. The caper *(Capparis sicula)* is a spiny shrub that grows in the hills around Jerusalem. The ancient Hebrews pickled the young buds and used them as a condiment. It is a plant often erroneously identified in the Bible as "hyssop," which is native to southern Europe and not to the eastern Mediterranean.

PICKLING CAPERS

To pickle your own capers, remove the stems from 2 cups of caper buds. Rinse the buds under running water. In a clean glass jar or glazed crock, alternate a layer of capers with a light layer of coarse sea salt or kosher salt. Let stand unrefrigerated, in a cool place, for 48 hours. Transfer to a sieve or colander, and rinse under running water. Drain, then return the buds to the glass jar or crock. In a pan, boil 1/4 cup water, 3/4 cup white wine vinegar, and 1 teaspoon salt. Pour over the capers. Cover and store in a cool place. Let stand for 2 weeks before using.

1 pound squash (bottle gourd,
   calabaza, opo squash, or
   zucchini), peeled (see Note)

1 cup water

1 clove garlic, minced

1 teaspoon salt

1/4 teaspoon freshly ground
   pepper

15 fresh mint leaves, finely
   chopped

1 tablespoon pickled caper juice

1 tablespoon red wine vinegar

2 tablespoons olive oil

1 tablespoon drained capers

Whole mint leaves

Cut the squash into small chunks. In a medium saucepan, combine the squash with the water. Bring to a boil and cook, covered, until the squash is tender, 10 to 15 minutes. Transfer to a colander to drain.

Place the squash in a medium bowl and mash with a fork. Add the garlic, salt, pepper, mint, caper juice, vinegar, and olive oil. Mix well. Transfer to a serving bowl, and sprinkle with capers. Garnish with whole mint leaves, and serve at room temperature.

Note: Opo, a spongy-fleshed squash with a pale green, slightly fuzzy skin, is available in Asian and gourmet markets.

Serves 4

MAIN MEALS

Basic Lamb/Beef Stock

Lamb and Lentil Stew

Chicken, Leek, and Garbanzo Bean Stew

Lamb and Fresh Fava Bean Stew

Goat, Squash, and Olive Stew

Jacob's Pottage of Lentils, Barley,
Mustard Greens, and Mint

Barley, Beef, and Onion Pottage

Three-Bean Pottage with Wheat Berries

Barley Gruel with Honey, Dates, and Raisins

Barley with Lentils and Onions

Pomegranate Honey–Glazed Grilled Fish

Cumin-Rubbed Roasted Lamb

Grilled Sardines with Fish Sauce

Grilled Quail

Basic Lamb/Beef Stock

Set on a pot, set it on, and also pour water into it:
Gather the pieces thereof into it, even every good piece, the thigh,
and the shoulder; fill it with the choice bones.
Take the choice of the flock, and burn also the bones under it, and make it
boil well, and let them seethe the bones of it therein.

Ezekiel 24:3–5

Much of the culinary language in the Bible is allegorical. In Ezekiel 24:3-5, it conveys a rather grim picture—the destruction of Jerusalem. Nevertheless, it describes a popular method of cooking in biblical times—that is, boiling or stewing. As described in Ezekiel 24:3–5, meat was commonly boiled or stewed, producing another sustaining food: stock. The ancient peoples of the Holy Land added chunks of lamb, goat, or beef to the pot, and seasoned it with onions, garlic, leeks, and wild herbs.

1¹/₂ pounds lamb bones or beef shortribs

1 whole onion, unpeeled

2 quarts water

3 leeks, green and white parts, cleaned and chopped

15 sprigs cilantro

6 sprigs dill

6 cloves garlic

1 bay leaf

5 black peppercorns

Salt to taste

Place the lamb bones, onion, water, and leeks in a large soup pot over medium-high heat. Tie the cilantro and dill together with cotton kitchen twine, and add them to the pot along with the garlic, bay leaf, and peppercorns. Cover the pot, and bring to a rolling boil. With a slotted spoon, skim off the foam. Decrease the heat to medium-low. Simmer until the broth reduces by at least one-third, 2 to 2¹/₂ hours.

Strain the stock through a fine-mesh strainer into a clean container. Let cool, then refrigerate for 4 to 6 hours or overnight. Skim off the fat and any other impurities that have risen to the top. Season with salt and use as directed or freeze for future use.

Makes about 5 cups

Lamb and Lentil Stew

*Butter of kine, and milk of sheep, with fat of lambs, and rams
of the breed of Bashan, and goats, with the fat of kidneys of wheat;
and thou didst drink the pure blood of the grape.*

DEUTERONOMY 32:14

Unlike modern, health-conscious consumers, the ancient Hebrews appreciated meats with a high fat content. This explains the popularity of fatted calf, stalled ox, and the fat-tailed sheep. The latter, with its wide, flat tail containing almost nothing but fat, was widely raised in biblical times. When available, such meat was most frequently prepared in a simple stew like this one. Served with a fresh loaf of Ezekiel's Bread (see page 71), this stew is a hearty meal.

1 pound lamb shoulder,
   cut into chunks

4 cloves garlic, slivered

2 tablespoons olive oil

6 pearl onions, peeled

3¹/₂ cups lamb/beef stock
   (see page 48)

1 tablespoon whole coriander
   seeds, toasted and ground
   (see pages 105, 107)

2 bay leaves

1 cup lentils, rinsed, drained,
   and picked over

Salt to taste

Freshly ground black pepper
   to taste

1 to 2 teaspoons wine vinegar or
   dry red wine (optional)

6 sprigs cilantro, leaves only

With a sharp knife, cut slits in the chunks of meat, and insert the garlic slivers.

In a heavy-bottomed casserole or stockpot, heat the olive oil over medium heat. Add the onions and cook, stirring occasionally, until they are lightly caramelized, 10 to 12 minutes. Add the meat and cook, stirring, until brown on all sides. Add the stock, coriander, and bay leaves. Cover and decrease the heat to medium-low. Cook until the meat is tender, 1¹/₄ to 1¹/₂ hours. Discard the bay leaves. With tongs, transfer the meat to a bowl. Cover to keep warm and set aside.

Add the lentils to the broth. Cover and cook until the lentils are tender, 20 to 25 minutes. Return the meat to the pot, and season with salt and pepper. Add the meat and heat through. Add the vinegar to the stew just before serving. Garnish with the cilantro and serve immediately.

Serves 4

Chicken, Leek, and Garbanzo Bean Stew

In the mountain of the height of Israel I will plant it;
and it shall bring forth boughs, and bear fruit, and be
a goodly cedar; and under it shall dwell all fowl of every wing
in the shadow of the branches thereof shall they dwell.

EZEKIEL 17:23

Domesticated hens were one of the "clean" or acceptable birds for Hebrews to eat, as mandated by Mosaic law. They were introduced from their native India around the time of Christ. Many farmers in the Holy Land raised poultry, either in the "free range" manner, or in enclosed areas. Serve this stew with warm bread or over cooked millet (see page 36).

2 large leeks

1/4 cup olive oil

1 1/2 pounds boneless, skinless chicken, cut into 2-inch pieces

1 1/2 cups garbanzo bean cooking liquid, water, or chicken broth

1 cup cooked garbanzo beans (see page 106)

3/4 teaspoon salt

1 teaspoon red wine vinegar

Trim the leeks, discarding the tough, outer leaves. Rinse thoroughly under running water. Cut the leeks crosswise into thin slices.

In a heavy pan, heat the olive oil over medium-high heat. Add the leeks and chicken, and cook, stirring occasionally, until the chicken turns golden brown, 8 to 10 minutes. Add the liquid. Cover and cook until the chicken is tender, 30 to 35 minutes. With a slotted spoon, transfer the chicken to a bowl, and set aside. Decrease the heat to low, and add the garbanzo beans. Simmer, uncovered, and reduce by one-third, 15 to 20 minutes. Season with salt and vinegar. Return the chicken to the pan and heat through. Serve immediately.

Serves 4

Lamb and Fresh Fava Bean Stew

*And on the eighth day he shall take two he lambs without blemish, and one
ewe lamb of the first year without blemish, and three tenth deals of fine
flour for a meat offering, mingled with oil, and one log of oil.*

LEVITICUS 14:10

Lamb was an important part of purification ceremonies performed by the temple priests. Goat, lamb, and mutton were also the most commonly eaten meats. This recipe combines lamb with fresh fava beans, another staple of the biblical diet. The ancient Hebrews most likely prepared stews like this one in heavy clay pots set over open fires and served them with hearty loaves like Ezekiel's Bread (see page 71). (Before you prepare fava beans, see the warning about favism on page 106.)

3 tablespoons olive oil

2 small onions, finely diced

2 pounds lamb shoulder or lamb breast, cut into 2-inch pieces

1¹/₂ cups water

3 cloves garlic, minced

2 pounds whole fresh fava beans, shelled (about 1³/₄ cups)

3 sprigs dill

1 teaspoon salt

In a Dutch oven or heavy-bottomed casserole, heat the olive oil over medium-high heat. Add the onions and cook, stirring occasionally, until golden, 6 to 8 minutes. Add the meat and cook, turning occasionally, until lightly browned, 10 to 12 minutes. Add 1 cup of the water and the garlic. Cover tightly, decrease the heat to medium-low, and cook until the meat is tender, 55 to 60 minutes. Meanwhile, peel the fava beans (see page 106).

When the meat is tender, add the favas, the remaining ¹/₂ cup water, and the dill. Cover and cook until the beans are tender, 15 to 20 minutes. Season with salt, and serve.

Serves 4

53

Goat, Squash, and Olive Stew

In scenes unchanged since the days of Gideon, solitary shepherds still watch over small flocks of sheep and goats grazing peacefully in the hills of the Holy Land. The ancient Hebrews raised goats for their milk; for their meat, which was less expensive than either mutton or beef; and for their skins, from which vessels for storing wine and water were made. Goat has a relatively strong flavor, and some consider it an acquired taste. If you are among them, substitute lamb or beef shortribs for the goat in this recipe. Any of the breads on pages 71–76 are perfect partners for this stew.

2 whole heads garlic, papery outer skin removed

1½ pounds goat ribs, cut into 2-inch pieces (see Note)

1 cup water

2 teaspoons coriander seeds, toasted and ground (see pages 105, 107)

15 sprigs cilantro, chopped

15 green olives, pitted

2 opo or zucchini squash, cut into 1-inch cubes (see Note)

Salt to taste

Freshly ground black pepper to taste

Preheat the oven to 350°. In a medium casserole or baking dish, nestle the heads of garlic among the pieces of meat. Add the water, coriander seeds, and cilantro. Cover tightly. Bake until the meat is partially cooked, 45 to 50 minutes. Remove the garlic.

Squeeze the head of garlic and collect the soft, buttery pulp. Return the garlic pulp to the dish, and mix it with the sauce. Add the olives and squash. Continue baking until the meat separates from the bones, 40 to 45 more minutes. Remove from the oven and drain the fat. Season with salt and pepper, and serve immediately.

Note: Goat meat is usually available in Asian and Mexican markets. For more about opo squash, see page 45.

Serves 4

54

And Gideon went in, and made ready a kid, and unleavened cakes
of an ephah of flour: the flesh he put in a basket, and he put
the broth in a pot, and brought it out unto him
under the oak, and presented it.

JUDGES 6:19

Jacob's Pottage of Lentils, Barley, Mustard Greens, and Mint

Then Jacob gave Esau bread and pottage of lentiles; and he did eat and drink, and rose up, and went his way: thus Esau despised his birthright.

GENESIS 25:34

Esau relinquished his birthright, the privilege and honor bestowed upon him as the first-born son, in return for some lentil stew. This hearty pottage of lentils, barley, and mustard greens seasoned with wild herbs may be similar to the one he was served. Although the ancient Hebrews cultivated the mustard plant primarily for its seed, it is likely that they enjoyed its peppery leaves as a potherb as well. Serve this stew with a loaf of fresh, warm bread, such as the ones on pages 71–76.

2 tablespoons olive oil

1 onion, diced

4 cloves garlic

2 tablespoons pearl barley

3/4 cup brown lentils, rinsed, drained, and picked over

1 leek, white part only, finely diced

6 cups lamb/beef stock (see page 48), or 3 (14 1/4-ounce) cans of broth

1 bunch mustard leaves, rinsed under running water, drained, and cut into thin ribbons

10 fresh mint leaves, finely chopped, or 2 teaspoons dried, crushed mint leaves

Salt to taste

Heat the olive oil in a large soup pot over medium-high heat. Cook the onion, stirring occasionally, until golden brown, 6 to 8 minutes. Add the garlic, barley, and lentils. Cook, while stirring, until the barley turns golden, 2 to 3 minutes. Add the leek and stock. Cover and cook, until the barley is tender, 30 to 35 minutes. Add the mustard leaves and cook until wilted, 2 to 3 minutes. Add the mint, season with salt, and serve immediately.

Serves 4 to 6

Barley, Beef, and Onion Pottage

*And I heard a voice in the midst of the four beasts say, A measure of wheat
for a penny, and three measures of barley for a penny...*

REVELATIONS 6:6

There are more than thirty references to barley in the Bible—indicative of its overall importance in the diet. Barley was far less expensive than wheat, which made it especially popular among the poor. Farmers could even afford to feed it to their cattle. Barley also served as a unit of measurement. Two barley corns set end-to-end were a "finger-breadth" and forty-eight, a "cubit" (16 inches by today's standards).

2 tablespoons olive oil

3 onions, chopped (about 2 cups)

1¹/₂ pounds beef shank meat, cubed

¹/₂ cup pearl barley, rinsed and drained

5 cups water

2 bay leaves

12 cloves garlic, peeled

Salt to taste

Freshly ground black pepper to taste

Heat the olive oil in a stockpot over medium-high heat. Add the onions and sauté, stirring, until they turn golden brown, 10 to 12 minutes. Add the meat and barley and cook, stirring, until the barley turns light brown, 5 to 6 minutes. Add the water, bay leaves, and garlic. Cover and decrease the heat to medium-low. Cook until the barley is soft, 55 to 60 minutes. Remove and discard the bay leaves. Season with salt and pepper, and serve immediately.

Serves 4

57

Three-Bean Pottage with Wheat Berries

Prove thy servants, I beseech thee, ten days;
and let them give us pulse to eat,
and water to drink.

DANIEL 1:12

It was common practice among the ancient Hebrews to eat roasted kernels of hulled wheat, which are referred to as "parched corn" in the King James Bible. We know these kernels as "wheat berries." When boiled, they acquire a pleasant chewiness similar to that of cooked whole barley, but have a nuttier flavor.

According to Harold Moldenke, Ph.D., and Alma Moldenke, authors of *Plants of the Bible,* five different varieties of wheat are native to the Holy Land. Even in biblical times, the region was reputed for its excellent wheat. Wheat and pulse (edible seeds of pod-bearing plants), like lentils and garbanzo beans, have been cultivated there since the earliest recorded time.

And they did eat of the old corn of the land
on the morrow after the passover, unleavened cakes,
and parched corn in the selfsame day.

JOSHUA 5:11

2 tablespoons olive oil

3 small onions, diced

$^1/_2$ cup dried fava beans, soaked and
   drained (see page 106)

$^1/_2$ cup dried garbanzo beans, soaked
   and drained (see page 106)

8 to 10 cups lamb/beef stock
   (see page 48), or 4 (14$^1/_4$-ounce)
   cans commercial broth

$^1/_2$ cup wheat berries

15 sprigs cilantro, tied with cotton
   kitchen string

4 cloves garlic

2 green onions, finely sliced

$^1/_2$ cup lentils, rinsed and drained

Salt to taste

Freshly ground black pepper to taste

In a large soup pot over medium-high, heat the olive oil and add the onions. Cook, stirring occasionally, until golden, 6 to 8 minutes. Add the favas and garbanzos, stock, wheat berries, cilantro, and garlic. Decrease the heat to medium. Cover and cook until the beans are tender, 2 to 2$^1/_2$ hours. Add the green onions and lentils and cook until the lentils are tender, 20 to 25 minutes. Remove and discard the cilantro. Season with salt and pepper, and serve immediately.

Serves 6 to 8

Barley Gruel with Honey, Dates, and Raisins

Then shall the man bring his wife unto the priest,
and he shall bring her offering for her,
the tenth part of an epah of barley meal;...

NUMBERS 5:15

Gruel's unsavory culinary reputation is undoubtedly a legacy of the "black bread and gruel" dungeon fare of centuries past. In fact, gruel is an ancient food whose preparation predates that of bread. It was an easily digested and nourishing dish of coarsely ground wheat, barley, millet, or spelt, cooked in water, milk, or broth. The dish was so common to the rations of Roman legionnaires, that Roman playwright Plautus has the Greek characters in his plays make fun of his own countrymen by calling them "gruel-eaters." Gruel could be a savory dish when mixed with onions, goat cheese, or salted fish; or a sweet one, with the addition of dates, raisins, or honey.

2¹/₂ cups cow's, goat's, or
   ewe's milk

2 teaspoons salt

2 tablespoons butter

2 cups instant barley grits
   (see Note)

4 pitted dates, coarsely chopped

2 tablespoons raisins, plumped
   in warm water and drained
   (see page 80)

Natural bee honey or fruit honey
   (see pages 93, 94, and 96)

Ground cinnamon, optional

In a large saucepan over medium-high heat, bring 2 cups of the milk, the salt, and butter to a boil. Add the barley grits, stir, and remove from the heat. Cover and let stand for 5 minutes. Stir in the dates and raisins. Spoon into individual bowls. Serve with the honey, cinnamon, and the remaining ¹/₂ cup milk on the side.

Note: Barley grits are available in the packaged cereal section of health food stores and gourmet markets.

Serves 4

Thy lips, O my spouse, drop as the honeycomb:
honey and milk are under thy tongue; and the smell
of thy garment is like the smell of Lebanon.
SONG OF SOLOMON 4:11

Barley with Lentils and Onions

And the flax and the barley was smitten:
for the barley was in the ear and the flax was bolled.

EXODUS 9:31

Barley is mentioned over thirty times in Scripture, thereby confirming its importance in the diet of the ancient Hebrews. It was frequently added, in its whole grain form or as barley cakes (see page 85), to thicken vegetarian and meat stews called "pottages." You can prepare this as a vegetarian dish, or add cooked lamb, chicken, or beef.

3 cups water

1/4 cup olive oil

1/4 teaspoon salt

1 garlic clove, coarsely chopped

1/2 cup pearl barley

1/2 cup lentils, rinsed and drained

1 bay leaf

2 large onions, finely diced

1 cup shredded cooked lamb,
    chicken, or beef (optional)

Salt to taste

Freshly ground black pepper
    to taste

In a medium saucepan, combine 1 1/2 cups of water, 2 tablespoons of the olive oil, the salt, and garlic. Bring to a boil and add the barley in a stream. Decrease the heat to medium, cover, and cook until the barley is tender, 40 to 45 minutes. Set aside.

In another medium saucepan, place the remaining 1 1/2 cups water, the lentils, and bay leaf. Cover and cook over medium heat until the lentils are tender, 15 to 20 minutes. Discard the bay leaf. Drain and set aside.

In a large skillet, heat the remaining 2 tablespoons olive oil over medium heat. Cook the onions, stirring occasionally, until they turn a deep golden brown, 30 to 35 minutes. Combine the barley, lentils, and meat (if using) with the onions. Cook, stirring, until hot. Season with salt and pepper. Serve immediately.

Serves 4

Pomegranate Honey—Glazed Grilled Fish

And they gave him a piece of a broiled fish, and of an honeycomb.

LUKE 24:42

In the time of Christ, the Sea of Galilee (Sea of Tiberias or Lake Gennesaret) was home to many species of fish. Religious Jews like Jesus and His disciples, who followed the dietary restrictions in Mosaic law, could only eat those varieties that had scales, which included several members of the carp family, the abundant Kinneret sardine (often preserved by pickling), and white musht, or *Tilapia galilea.*

Mendel Nun, a fisherman, biblical scholar, and author, who resides on the shores of the Sea of Galilee, believes that tilapia, or "St. Peter's Fish," as it is commonly known, was the fish with which Jesus fed the multitudes. It is the same fish that Peter caught in such quantities that they caused his net to "brake" (tear). The firm, white flesh of tilapia fillets is perfect for grilling.

1/4 cup olive oil

1 tablespoon Pomegranate Honey
(see page 94)

2 teaspoons red wine vinegar

1 clove garlic, minced

Salt to taste

1 1/2 pounds tilapia (see Note),
cleaned, scaled, and filleted

Prepare a charcoal fire. Brush the grill lightly with olive oil.

In a small bowl, mix the olive oil, Pomegranate Honey, vinegar, garlic, and salt. With a pastry brush, coat the fish with the mixture.

Grill until the flesh is flaky and looses its translucence, 3 to 4 minutes on each side. Serve immediately.

Note: Today, tilapia is one of the world's most common farm-raised fish. It is sold live in Asian supermarkets and fresh or frozen in most others.

Serves 2

Cumin-Rubbed Roasted Lamb

And they shall eat the flesh in that night,
roast with fire, and unleavened bread; and with
bitter herbs they shall eat it.

EXODUS 12:8

Here in the Bible, God gives His instructions for the preparation of paschal lamb to Moses and Aaron. The ancient Hebrews believed that the aromatic smoke from "meat roasted with fire" was pleasing to God. It certainly must have been pleasing to them as well, for meat, especially when roasted, was considered a luxury usually reserved for special occasions and religious celebrations like Passover. Although this recipe calls for trimming the fat from the leg of lamb, the ancient Hebrews certainly would not have done so. They loved fat!

3 tablespoons extra virgin olive oil

2 cloves garlic, minced

1 teaspoon cumin seeds, toasted
and ground (see pages 105, 107)

5-pound leg of lamb, trimmed
of fat

Salt to taste

Freshly ground black pepper
to taste

Preheat oven to 500°.

In a small mixing bowl, combine the olive oil, garlic, and cumin to make a paste. With a pastry brush or your hands, spread the paste all over the leg of lamb. Sprinkle with salt and pepper. Set the lamb in a baking dish. Insert a meat thermometer in the leg of lamb, making sure it doesn't come into contact with the bone. Place the lamb in the oven and roast until a brown crust forms, 12 to 15 minutes. Decrease the heat to 350° and continue roasting for 1 hour 15 minutes to 1$^{1}/_{2}$ hours, or until you cut into the thickest part of the leg and see the meat is cooked to your liking. The meat thermometer will register between 135° (for rare) and 160° (for well done).

Unleavened Griddle Bread
(see page 74)

Bitter herbs (such as arugula,
chicory, dandelion, endive,
sorrel, or watercress), washed
and dried

Alternately, roast the lamb on a grill. Prepare a charcoal fire in a large, lidded barbecue. Coat the lamb with the savory paste and season with salt and pepper, as instructed for the roasting method.

Using a fireproof utensil, move the hot charcoal to the perimeter of the barbecue basin. Place a shallow drip pan in the center of the rack. Set the lamb in the pan. Lower the lid and open the vents about 1 inch. Roast for 1 hour 15 minutes to 1 hour 45 minutes, or until you cut into the thickest part of the leg and see the meat is cooked to your liking. The meat thermometer will register between 135° (for rare) and 160° (for well done).

Transfer the lamb to a platter and let stand 10 to 15 minutes before carving. Pour the pan juices over the meat, slice, and serve with the bread and bitter herbs (to sop up the juices).

Serves 6

Grilled Sardines with Fish Sauce

As soon then as they were come to land, they saw a fire of coals there,
and fish laid thereon, and bread.

JOHN 21:9

Fish, both freshwater and saltwater varieties, were an important dietary supplement for the ancient Hebrews. When preserved in salt and dried, fish was an object of commerce, exported as far as Rome. Tyrian merchants brought some of their catch to sell near Jerusalem's "Fish Gate." No doubt, they also imported a pungent, fermented condiment that the Romans called *garum* (probably similar to Vietnamese nuoc mam). First-century Roman writer Apicius included it in several sweet and savory recipes in his cookbook *Apicius de re Coquinaria*.

1/4 cup olive oil, plus extra for brushing grill

1 garlic clove, finely chopped

1 small onion, diced

1 tablespoon Vietnamese fish sauce (nuoc mam, see Note)

3 tablespoons water

1 tablespoon white wine vinegar

1 tablespoon honey

Freshly ground black pepper to taste

8 medium sardines, scaled, gutted, and washed

Brush the grill rack with olive oil and prepare a charcoal fire.

In a small saucepan, heat 2 teaspoons of the olive oil. Add the garlic and the onion, stirring occasionally, until soft, 3 to 4 minutes. Add the fish sauce, water, vinegar, and honey. Stir until the honey is dissolved. Season with pepper. Remove from the heat and keep warm.

Pat the sardines dry, and coat them with the remaining olive oil. Place them on the grill and cook until the skin turns crispy and the flesh is firm, 3 to 4 minutes on each side. Serve immediately with the warm, seasoned fish sauce on the side.

Note: Vietnamese fish sauce (nuoc mam) is available in Asian markets.

Serves 4

Grilled Quail

Thou didst prepare quails to eat a delicacy to satisfy a desire of appetite.

SONG OF SOLOMON 16:2

And it came to pass, that as even the quails came up, and covered the camp:
and in the morning the dew lay round the host.

EXODUS 16:13

God sent quail and manna to sustain his people as they wandered in the wilderness following their flight from Egypt. The diminutive quail was, and still is, a popular delicacy in the eastern Mediterranean. It is especially abundant during the birds' annual migration across the Sinai Desert. Eat quail the way the ancient Hebrews would have: with your fingers.

2 tablespoons olive oil, plus extra for brushing grill

1 clove garlic, minced

4 quail, rinsed and patted dry

Salt to taste

Freshly ground black pepper to taste

Prepare a charcoal fire. Brush the grill lightly with olive oil.

In a small bowl, mix the olive oil with the garlic. Lightly coat the quail with the mixture. Sprinkle the birds lightly with salt and pepper inside and out.

Grill about 4 inches away from the coals, turning occasionally with tongs, until the juices run clear, 10 to 12 minutes. Serve immediately.

Note: Fresh quail are available from specialty butchers. Frozen quail are often available in Asian supermarkets.

Serves 4

BREADS AND DESSERTS

Sourdough Starter

Ezekiel's Bread

Unleavened Griddle Bread

Leavened Griddle Bread

Dried Fruit, Cinnamon, and
Red Wine Compote (Harosset)

Sundried Raisins

Abigail's Fig Cakes

Apricots with Pomegranate Seeds and
Toasted Nuts in Honey Syrup

Almond and Honey–Filled Dates

Barley Cakes

Sourdough Starter

…Know ye not that a little leaven will leaveneth the whole loaf?

1 CORINTHIANS 5:7

Naturally occurring wild yeasts were the first leavening agents used in the preparation of bread. The ancient Hebrews certainly did not understand the biochemical process whereby microscopic fungi from the ambient air caused the starch in their flour and water mixtures to ferment. Empirically, however, they knew it worked. Like bakers in the Holy Land two thousand years ago, modern cooks may not be successful every time they attempt to make sourdough starter. For a source of 100 percent reliable, commercial sourdough starter, see page 109.

3 cups white bread flour

4 cups warm water (75° to 80°)

In a large glass jar, blend 1 cup of the flour with 2 cups of the water. Cover with fine gauze or cheesecloth and set in a draft-free, warm place to proof.

On the second day, bubbles should begin to form. This means that yeast cells from the air have been successfully trapped in the dough. Add $^1/_2$ cup of the remaining flour and $^1/_2$ cup of the remaining water and mix well. Repeat this step for the next 3 days. By this time, a spongelike layer, 1 to 2 inches thick, should have formed over the top of the liquid. Stir the starter and use as directed in the following recipes.

To keep the yeast in the remaining starter active for future bread baking, continue to add flour and water in $^1/_2$-cup increments every day. To temporarily halt the action of the yeast, simply refrigerate the starter. Bring the starter to room temperature before using. Should the spongelike layer of dough fail to reappear at the top of your starter, discard it and start over.

Makes about 6 cups

Ezekiel's Bread

Take thou also unto thee wheat, and barley, and beans, and lentiles,
and millet, and fitches, and put them in one vessel, and make thee bread
thereof, according to the number of the days that thou shalt lie
upon thy side, three hundred and ninety days shalt thou eat thereof.

EZEKIEL 4:9

The prophet Ezekiel's "recipe" was meant to teach the ancient inhabitants of Jerusalem to use every available food during the impending Babylonian siege of their city. Bread was more than physical nourishment for the people of the Old and New Testaments—it held symbolic meaning as well. Just as individual grains are bound together to form bread, so the act of sharing bread bound one man to another, establishing a sacred covenant among those who shared it.

For the most part, it was the woman of the household who baked the bread for her family. However, the reference to a "bakers' street" in Jeremiah 37:21 indicates there must have also been a commercial source for obtaining one's daily bread.

The ancient bread bakers frequently combined wheat flour with other coarsely or finely ground grains and pulses, like millet, fitches (probably spelt, an ancient variety of wheat), barley, fava beans, and lentils. For leavening, they used a piece of yeast-fermented dough set aside from the previous day's batch.

And the floors shall be of wheat,
and the vats shall overflow with wine and oil.

JOEL 2:24

71

(continued)

(continued from previous page)

1 tablespoon plus 2 teaspoons
   active dry yeast

1¹/₂ cups warm water
   (105° to 110°)

3 cups white bread flour

1³/₄ cups stoneground spelt flour
   (see Note)

¹/₂ cup barley flour

¹/₄ cup lentils, finely ground
   (see page 105)

¹/₄ cup dried fava beans, finely
   ground (see page 106)

1 tablespoon millet

1 tablespoon salt

¹/₄ cup plus 2 tablespoons olive oil

3 tablespoons bee honey or Date
   Honey (see page 96)

¹/₂ cup barley grits

1 tablespoon nigella seeds (see
   Note, see page 26), or toasted,
   coarsely crushed coriander
   seeds (see page 107)

In a small bowl, dissolve the yeast in ¹/₄ cup of the water. Let stand until the mixture starts to bubble, 10 to 15 minutes. Alternatively, substitute 4 cups of Sourdough Starter (see page 70) for the yeast and water.

In a large mixing bowl, combine the white bread, spelt, and barley flours, ground lentils and fava beans, millet, and salt. Stir to blend, and make a well in the center. Pour the yeast mixture, ¹/₄ cup of the olive oil, and the honey into the well. Mix thoroughly, adding the remaining water 2 tablespoons at a time, until a loose dough forms. Transfer the dough to a floured work surface, and knead until the dough feels elastic to the touch, 10 to 12 minutes. Shape the dough into a large ball. Cover it with a kitchen towel, and let rest for 3 to 4 minutes.

Vigorously knead the dough for 1 more minute. Lightly grease two baking sheets and sprinkle them generously with the barley grits. Divide the dough into two equal portions. Set them on the baking sheets. With your fingers, pat the dough into 8-inch circles. Cover each loaf with a kitchen towel. Set them aside in a draft-free, warm area (75° to 80°). Let the loaves rise until they double in size.

Preheat the oven to 400°. With a small pastry brush or your hands, coat each loaf with the remaining 2 tablespoons olive oil. Sprinkle with nigella. Bake the loaves until they are crusty and brown, and the undersides sounds hollow when tapped, 40 to 45 minutes.

Note: A baking stone yields an especially crusty bread. To use, place the stone directly on the lower oven rack and preheat it along with the oven for 15 to 20 minutes. Sprinkle the hot stone lightly with barley grits. Transfer the risen bread to the stone, and follow the directions above.

Spelt flour is available in some health food stores and gourmet markets, or it can be purchased through the mail (see page 108).

Makes two 10-inch round loaves

*It is like leaven, which a woman took
and hid in three measures of meal,
till the whole was leavened.*

LUKE 13:21

Unleavened Griddle Bread

Seven days shall ye eat unleavened bread; even the first day ye shall put away leaven out of your houses: for whosoever eateth leavened bread from the first day until the seventh day, that soul shall be cut off from Israel.

EXODUS 12:15

In the first month, on the fourteenth day of the month at even, ye shall eat unleavened bread, until the one and twentieth day of the month at even.

EXODUS 12:18

Bread was the staple of the biblical diet. In times of hardship, it was the only food available to the ancient Hebrews. They believed that bread was in its natural state when "uncorrupted by leaven." For this reason, it was the only bread sanctioned for sacred occasions. God directed His chosen people to commemorate their freedom from bondage in Egypt by eating unleavened bread from the fourteenth to the twenty-first day during the month of Passover. As a token offering on every sabbath, the priests placed twelve loaves of unleavened bread called "shewbread" on the temple's altar.

Both for the shewbread, and for the fine flour for meat offering, and for the unleavened cakes, and for that which is baked in the pan, and for that which is fried...

1 CHRONICLES 23:29

And unleavened bread, and cakes unleavened tempered with oil,
and wafers unleavened anointed with oil: of wheaten flour
shalt thou make them.

EXODUS 29:2

1 cup whole-wheat flour

2 cups white bread flour

2 teaspoons salt

1 cup 2 tablespoons water

1 tablespoon nigella seeds
(see Note, page 26), or toasted
and cracked coriander or
toasted cumin seeds
(see page 107)

Olive oil for cooking

In a large bowl, combine the whole-wheat and white bread flours. Add salt and blend. Make a well in the center. Gradually add the water, and mix thoroughly until a loose dough forms. Transfer the mixture to a lightly floured work surface. Knead until the dough becomes soft and elastic, 10 to 12 minutes. Shape the dough into a ball and let it rest for 15 to 30 minutes. Knead it again, vigorously, for 1 minute.

Preheat a cast-iron pan or griddle over medium-high heat. Separate the dough into 8 equal balls. On a floured surface, roll out each ball of dough to a diameter of 6 inches and a thickness of $1/8$ inch. Sprinkle the tops with nigella seeds. Using the rolling pin, roll the seeds into the top of the dough. Lightly coat the pan or griddle with the oil. Place the bread rounds in the pan or on the griddle, and cook until each round is dotted with dark brown spots and puffs slightly, 2 to 3 minutes per side. Stack on a plate and serve warm.

Makes eight 6-inch breads

Leavened Griddle Bread

And wine that maketh glad the heart of man, and oil to make
his face to shine, and bread which strengtheneth man's heart.

PSALMS 104:15

Grain from primitive varieties of cereal grasses has been harvested and consumed by peoples of the eastern Mediterranean since prehistoric times. They first ate it parched (roasted over an open flame) or mixed with water as a thin gruel. Later, the art of bread making developed. By the time of the Old Testament, bakers had learned to produce leavened, unleavened, and multigrain bread, which they cooked directly on hot stones, in pans or griddles, or in earthen ovens. More than any other food, it was bread that sustained God's chosen people. Wine may "maketh glad the heart of man," but bread "strengtheneth man's heart." These breads are especially good served warm with Leek Dip (see page 25) or any of the fruit honeys on pages 93–96.

And he looked, and, behold, there was a cake baken
on the coals, and a cruse of water at his head....

1 KINGS 19:6

1¹/₂ teaspoons active dry yeast

1¹/₄ cups warm water
(105° to 110°)

1 cup white bread flour

2 cups stoneground whole-wheat
flour

2 teaspoons salt

2 tablespoons olive oil, plus more
for cooking

In a small bowl, dissolve the yeast in ¹/₄ cup of the water. Let stand until the mixture starts to bubble, 10 to 15 minutes.

In a large mixing bowl, combine the white bread flour, whole-wheat flour, and salt. Stir to blend, and make a well in the center. Pour the yeast mixture and the olive oil into the well. Mix thoroughly, adding the remaining water, 2 tablespoons at a time, until a loose dough forms. Transfer the dough to a floured work surface, and knead until the dough feels elastic to the touch, 10 to 12 minutes. Let the dough rest for 3 to 4 minutes, then vigorously knead it again for 1 minute. Shape the dough into a large ball. Lightly oil a bowl, and place the dough in it. Cover with a clean cloth, and let the dough rise until it has doubled in size, 2 to 4 hours.

Preheat a heavy, cast-iron pan or griddle over medium-high heat. Divide the dough into 8 equal portions. Sprinkle the work surface lightly with flour. With the tips of your fingers, flatten each piece into ¹/₄-inch-thick, 6-inch-diameter rounds.

Lightly brush the pan or griddle with olive oil. Place the bread rounds in the pan or on the griddle and cook until each bread is dotted with dark brown spots and rises slightly, 2 to 3 minutes per side. Stack on a plate, and serve warm.

Makes eight 6-inch breads

Dried Fruit, Cinnamon, and Red Wine Compote (Harosset)

And their father Israel said unto them,
If it must be so now, do this; take of the best fruits in the land
in your vessels, and carry down the man a present,
a little balm, and a little honey, spices, and myrrh, nuts, and almonds…

GENESIS 43:11

Ancient Arab and Phoenician traders imported cinnamon to the Holy Land from the island known today as Sri Lanka. In Exodus 30:23, Moses used cinnamon to perfume the holy oil with which he anointed the sacred vessels in the temple. The exotic spice also lent its distinctive fragrance and flavor to this blend of dried fruits and nuts called *harosset*, which is served in Jewish homes during the celebration of Passover. The mixture of hard and soft ingredients symbolizes the brick and clay building materials used by enslaved Hebrew workers during their bondage in Egypt.

Take thou also unto thee principal spices, of pure myrrh five hundred
shekels, and of sweet cinnamon half so much, even two hundred and fifty
shekels, and of sweet calamus two hundred and fifty shekels…

EXODUS 30:23

8 ounces dried apricots

8 ounces pitted dates, finely chopped

4 ounces dried Mission figs, coarsely chopped (about ³/4 cup)

4 ounces raisins (about ³/4 cup)

1³/4 cups sweet red kosher wine or port

1 teaspoon ground cinnamon

¹/2 cup crushed almonds, pistachios, or walnuts

Whole nuts for garnish

Soak the apricots in warm water until plumped, about 30 minutes. Drain and finely chop.

Place the dates, apricots, figs, raisins, wine, and cinnamon in a saucepan. Cook over medium heat, stirring, until the mixture thickens. Add the crushed nuts, and stir to blend.

Spread the mixture on a shallow platter. Garnish with whole nuts, and serve. Supply each guest with a spoon to eat from the communal dish.

Serves 4 to 6

Sundried Raisins

Moreover they that were nigh them, even unto Issachar and Zebulun and
Naphtali, brought bread on asses, and on camels, and on mules, and
on oxen, and meat, meal, cakes of figs, and bunches of raisins, and wine,
and oil, and oxen, and sheep abundantly: for there was joy in Israel.

1 CHRONICLES 12:40

The finest grapes harvested from biblical vineyards were dried in the sun to produce raisins. Like dried figs, they were commonly pressed into cakes—simple, practical, and fortifying snacks for workmen and travelers. In 1 Samuel 30:11–12, David gives a cluster of raisins and a cake of figs to a famished Egyptian boy to help restore his strength.

1 pound large red seedless grapes, washed

Remove the grapes' stems. Place the grapes on a baking sheet. Cover with a fine-mesh screen or cheesecloth. Set them out in the full sun each day, bringing them in at night, until the grapes become dehydrated and dark red-black in color. This process can take up to 1 week.

Makes about ¼ cup

Abigail's Fig Cakes

Then Abigail made haste, and took two hundred loaves,
and two bottles of wine, and five sheep ready dressed, and five measures
of parched corn, and an hundred clusters of raisins,
and two hundred cakes of figs, and laid them on asses.

1 SAMUEL 25:18

In 1 Samuel 25:18, Abigail is preparing to deliver a culinary peace offering to David, who has been insulted by her husband Nabal. Her quick thinking, sage advice to David, and, perhaps in some small part, her delicious fig cakes worked so well that, following Nabal's death, David took her for his wife!

20 dried golden Smyrna or
   Calimyrna figs

6 ounces walnuts or almonds, lightly
   toasted and coarsely ground
   (see pages 105, 107)

1 teaspoon ground cinnamon

In a medium bowl filled with warm water, soak the figs for 2 to 4 hours. Drain and finely chop the figs (you should have about 2¼ cups).

Lightly grease a baking sheet. In a medium bowl, mix the figs with the crushed nuts and cinnamon. Shape 1 heaping tablespoon of the mixture into a patty about 1½ inches in diameter and ½ inch thick. Set the patty on the baking sheet. Repeat until the entire mixture has been used.

Preheat the oven to 200°. Bake the cakes until they become moderately dry, 2 to 3 hours. Let cool completely before serving. Store at room temperature in a tightly sealed container.

81

Makes 20 to 22 cakes

Apricots with Pomegranate Seeds and Toasted Nuts in Honey Syrup

Thy plants are an orchard of pomegranates,
with pleasant fruits; camphire, with spikenard…

SONG OF SOLOMON 4:13

Prominent biblical botanists now believe that Eve tempted Adam with an apricot, and not an apple. The apricot was introduced to the Holy Land almost 3,000 years before Christ and grows there in abundance today. The ancient Hebrews would have dried a portion of their sweet, early summer crop for use later in the year—in late fall, for example, when they could mix it with fresh, ripe, pomegranate seeds.

I went down into the garden of nuts to see the fruits of the valley,
and to see whether the vine flourished, and the pomegranates budded.

SONG OF SOLOMON 6:11

¹/₂ cup honey

¹/₃ cup water

1 (1-inch-long) cinnamon stick

3 tablespoons sweet red wine

16 large, dried apricot halves,
  plumped in hot water for
  30 minutes and drained

1 pomegranate, seeded
  (see page 107)

¹/₃ cup chopped pistachios or
  sliced almonds, toasted
  (see page 107)

In a medium saucepan, bring the honey, water, cinnamon stick, and wine to a low boil. Add the apricots and poach them until they are soft, 15 to 20 minutes. Discard the cinnamon stick and let the mixture cool.

Reserving the syrup in the saucepan, transfer the apricots to a wide, shallow serving bowl and arrange them so they are hollow-side up. Top each one with pomegranate seeds. Spoon the reserved syrup over the top and sprinkle with nuts. Serve at room temperature.

Serves 4

Almond and Honey—Filled Dates

And he will take your daughters to be confectionaries,
and to be cooks, and to be bakers...

GENESIS 40:2

Since antiquity, dates have been one of the principal foods of the peoples of the Holy Land. Biblical botanists believe that at one time the Jordan River Valley was a virtual forest of palms. This explains why Jericho, near the river's southern end, five miles north of the Dead Sea, was described as the "city of palms trees" in Deuteronomy 34:3. The ancient Hebrews ate the sweet fruit from the fall harvest in its natural state, or used it in confections like this one.

3/4 cup sesame seeds, toasted
(see page 107)

1 cup whole almonds, coarsely
ground

1 cup honey

15 medium Medjool dates,
halved lengthwise and pitted
(see Note)

Place the sesame seeds in a medium bowl.

In a saucepan over medium-low heat, warm the honey until it becomes foamy, 8 to 10 minutes. Remove from the heat. Stir in the almonds, then let the mixture cool until the honey is the consistency of soft caramel.

Scoop up a heaping teaspoon of the almond-honey mixture. With your fingertips, roll it in the sesame seeds until well coated, then gently stuff the sesame seed-coated mixture into a date half. Set aside. Repeat until all the date halves are filled. Store in a covered container in a cool place until ready to serve.

Note: See page 109 for a source for medium-size Medjool dates.

Makes about 30

Barley Cakes

…Behold, I dreamed a dream, and lo, a cake of barley bread tumbled into the host of Midian, and came into a tent, and smote it that it fell, and overturned it, that the tent lay along.

JUDGES 7:13

The dream described in Judges 7:13 was an omen of victory for Gideon. His forces of agrarian Hebrews (symbolized by the barley cake) would score a decisive victory over the nomadic Midianite enemy (symbolized by the tent). Barley was a staple of the ancient Hebrew diet, especially among the common people. Barley kernels were coarsely ground into meal for gruel, or finely ground into flour for bread making. The "cakes" in this recipe were eaten out of hand or used to thicken stews.

1¹/₂ cups water or milk

2 tablespoons olive oil or butter

¹/₄ teaspoon salt

1 cup barley grits

Ground cinnamon

1 cup honey, slightly warmed

In a medium saucepan, bring the water, 1 tablespoon of the olive oil, and the salt to a boil. Decrease the heat to medium. Add the barley grits in a stream. Stir once and cover. Cook until the barley is tender, 12 to 15 minutes. Meanwhile, lightly oil an 8 x 8-inch pan. Transfer the barley to the prepared pan. With a spatula, spread the barley evenly in the pan and set aside to cool.

Using your hands, shape the barley mixture into 6 "cakes" of equal size. Heat the remaining tablespoon of olive oil in a large frying pan over medium heat. Add the cakes and cook until golden, 5 to 6 minutes on each side. Sprinkle lightly with the cinnamon, then serve immediately with the warm honey on the side.

Makes 6

BASICS AND BEVERAGES

Goat's Milk Cheese

Homemade Yogurt

Herb-Coated Yogurt Cheese

Grape Honey

Pomegranate Honey

Date Honey

Homemade Red Wine

New Wine (or Fresh Grape Juice)

Vinegar

Spiced Pomegranate Wine

Goat's Milk Cheese

Hast thou not poured me out as milk,
and curdled me like cheese?

JOB 10:10

Dairy products were plentiful in the "land of milk and honey." The ancient Hebrews probably consumed milk (especially from sheep and goats) on a daily basis. Surplus milk was transformed into nourishing foods like butter, yogurt, and cheese. These could be preserved underground in clay jars or, in the case of yogurt and cheese, rolled in salt and dried in the sun. The ancient peoples of the Near East must have had an empirical understanding of rennet, an enzyme extracted from the stomachs of young calves or lambs, which is still used in the production of certain cheeses. A form of rennet is also present in the juice of fig leaves and in some varieties of thistles and melons. In this recipe, however, we follow an acid-cure method, using acetic acid, for curdling goat's milk. My friend Suhama Mansour, a Chaldean immigrant to the United States, remembers how her grandmother did just this, using a little date vinegar to curdle milk. I have substituted white wine vinegar in the following recipe. You will need a large square piece of clean, white cotton cloth (such as a cotton napkin or a piece of fine muslin) for straining the milk and some cotton kitchen string.

1 quart goat's milk (see Note)

2 tablespoons white wine vinegar

2 teaspoons kosher salt, plus
    additional for preserving

2 teaspoons chopped dill

In a large saucepan over medium heat, bring the milk to a slow boil. Add the vinegar, stirring continuously with a wooden spoon, until the milk is curdled, 3 to 4 minutes. Remove the pan from the heat, and stir in the 2 teaspoons salt. Let stand for 2 minutes.

Line a colander with white cotton cloth. Pour the milk in the center, gather up the corners, twist the cloth to extract some of the whey, and tie with kitchen string. Place in the colander and allow it to drain for 2 to 3 hours.

When most of the whey has drained out, place the curd-filled sack on a flat board or a large plate. Set it on a gentle slope so any remaining whey can drain off. Compress the sack with a heavy, flat object, such as a kettle filled with water. Let it stand for 8 to 10 hours, or overnight, on the kitchen counter. At this point, the curds will have attained the consistency of whipped cream cheese. With a rubber spatula, scrape the cheese into a bowl.

With your hands, fashion the cheese into a small patty. Lightly sprinkle salt all over it, and roll it in chopped dill. Cover and refrigerate. Consume the cheese within 3 to 4 days.

Note: You can, of course, substitute cow's or sheep's milk for the goat's milk in this recipe.

Makes one 5-ounce cheese

89

Homemade Yogurt

And he took butter, and milk, and the calf which he had dressed,
and set it before them; and he stood by them
under the tree, and they did eat.

GENESIS 18:8

In Genesis 18:8, Abraham presents the three angels with butter. According to a recent edition of the New American Bible, however, it was curd, "a type of soft cheese or yogurt." Fermented milk products like these originated in the Middle East. Many people there still follow the same age-old method as Sarah, Abraham's wife, when making yogurt from the milk of sheep, goats, or cows. They usually set aside a small portion of curd to use as starter for the next batch. Use a bit of commercial yogurt to get the initial batch started.

1 quart whole sheep's, goat's,
  or cow's milk

1 tablespoon unpasteurized
  plain yogurt

In a large pan over medium heat, scald the milk until a soft foam forms on the surface. Remove the pan from the heat and transfer the milk to a large glass bowl. Set aside to cool.

When the milk is cool enough to comfortably dip a finger into, add the yogurt, 1 teaspoon at a time, to different parts of the bowl. Stir once. Cover the bowl with a clean kitchen towel and place it in a warm, dry place, away from drafts (such as in the oven of a gas stove with the pilot light turned on, or in an electric oven that has been preheated for about 1 minute). Do not disturb the mixture, or it will not curdle (thicken) as it sours. Let stand for 10 to 12 hours. Cover and refrigerate. Consume within 3 to 4 days.

Makes 1 quart

VARIATION
Homemade Yogurt with Natural Starter

Let 1 quart of milk stand at room temperature overnight or longer, until it curdles and attains a thick, creamy consistency. At this point, drain the yogurt into fine cheesecloth, and discard the whey (watery residue). What remains is yogurt and is ready to eat. Save some as a starter to seed the next batch.

In a saucepan over medium heat, bring 2 more cups of milk to a simmer. When the milk begins to foam, remove it from the heat and transfer it to a glass or earthenware bowl. Set aside to cool.

When the milk is cool enough to comfortably dip a finger into, add the starter. Stir once. Cover the bowl with a plate, and set it aside in a warm place, away from drafts. (You can also double-wrap the bowl in a bath towel or blanket.) Do not disturb the mixture, or it will not curdle. Let stand for 10 to 12 hours. Discard the whey. Refrigerate until ready to use.

Makes 1 quart

Herb-Coated Yogurt Cheeses

*And carry these ten cheeses unto the captain of their thousand,
and look how thy brethren fare, and take their pledge.*

1 SAMUEL 17:18

Jesse commanded his son David to deliver "cheeses" to the officer preparing to do battle with Goliath and the Philistines. It may well have been this yogurt cheese. In the Holy Land, it is still produced by draining off the whey from soured milk or yogurt. The resulting product has the consistency of cream cheese and can be used as a spread. It can also be shaped into small balls and rolled in aromatic herbs, like dill or green onion. Keep them in the refrigerator, or preserved in olive oil or salt brine. You will need some cotton kitchen string and a large, square piece of clean white cotton cloth for draining the yogurt.

**2 cups Homemade Yogurt
(see page 90)**

**2 tablespoons finely chopped dill
or green onion**

**Virgin olive oil or salt brine
(see page 30, optional)**

Line a colander with fine, clean, white cotton cloth. Pour the yogurt into the center, gather up the corners, twist the cloth to extract some of the whey, and tie with string. Drain for 18 to 24 hours. The yogurt cheese should have a soft consistency, yet be firm enough to shape into balls.

Shape the yogurt cheese into small balls and roll them in the dill or green onion. Refrigerate until ready to serve, or store in a clean jar and cover with olive oil or salt brine.

*Makes 5 yogurt cheese balls
or 6 ounces yogurt cheese*

Grape Honey

…In my dream, behold, a vine was before me; and in the vine there were
three branches; and it was as though it budded, and her blossoms shot forth;
and the clusters thereof brought forth ripe grapes…

GENESIS 40:9–10

Grapes were as plentiful in the Holy Land as they were in the vineyards of ancient Egypt. Although the best grapes were made into raisins, the bulk of the harvest was delivered to rock-cut winepresses where the grapes were crushed underfoot. The ancient Hebrews drank some of the fresh juice or "new wine" that drained off. The rest they transferred to vessels for natural fermentation and wine production, or boiled down into a sweet, viscous syrup called grape honey. Serve this honey as a condiment or dip for wedges of warm Unleavened Griddle Bread (see page 74) or Leavened Griddle Bread (see page 76), or blend it with equal parts of almond butter, pistachio butter, or sesame butter (tahini) to create an unusual spread for flatbread.

$3^{1}/_{2}$ **pounds sweet grapes,**
washed and patted dry

Remove the stems. In a large bowl, mash the grapes and squeeze them with your hands. Strain them through a large fine-mesh sieve set over a bowl, pressing with the back of a wooden spoon to extract as much juice as possible. Discard the skins and seeds. The grapes should yield about $4^{1}/_{2}$ cups of juice.

Pour the juice into a nonreactive saucepan. Over medium heat, bring the juice to a gentle simmer and cook until it has the consistency of molten honey, 1 to $1^{1}/_{2}$ hours. Remove from the heat and let cool. Transfer to a glass jar with a tight-fitting lid and store in the refrigerator. The honey will keep for up to 3 months.

Makes about $^{1}/_{2}$ cup

93

Pomegranate Honey

Let us get up early to the vineyards; let us see if the vine flourish,
whether the tender grape appear, and the pomegranates
bud forth: there will I give thee my loves.

SONG OF SOLOMON 7:12

The spiny pomegranate shrub grew prolifically throughout the Holy Land. Its fruit, symbolic of fertility, was well known to the people of the Old Testament, especially the Tyrian master craftsman Huram, from the First Book of Kings, who created hundreds of bronze pomegranates to decorate the capitals that sat atop the columns at the entrance to King Solomon's palace. Pomegranates in blue, gold, and purple also adorned the ephods (robes) worn by the temple priests. The ancient Hebrews ate the ripe seeds of the ruby-skinned fruit, drank its tart juice (which they also fermented into a heady wine), or produced a thick, concentrated, sweet-sour syrup. It is marketed as pomegranate molasses in Middle Eastern markets. Use it as a marinade or a condiment or as a dip for wedges of Unleavened Griddle Bread (see page 74) or Leavened Griddle Bread (see page 76). Or, blend it with equal parts of almond butter, pistachio butter, and sesame butter (tahini) to create an unusual spread for flatbread.

8 cups pomegranate seeds
   (from about 8 large
   pomegranates; see page 107
   and Note, below)

Using a mortar and pestle, a food mill, or a food processor, mash the pomegranate seeds. Strain through a medium-mesh sieve set over a bowl. Strain again through a fine-mesh sieve, pressing the pulp with the back of a wooden spoon to extract as much juice as possible. Discard the pulp. Pour the juice into a nonreactive saucepan. Over medium heat, bring the juice to a gentle simmer and cook until it is the consistency of molten honey, 1 to 1^1/$_2$ hours. Remove from the heat and let cool. Transfer to a glass jar with a tight-fitting lid and store in the refrigerator. The honey will keep for up to 3 months.

Note: If fresh pomegranates are not in season, you can purchase bottles of pomegranate juice in Middle Eastern markets or health food stores. Do not substitute grenadine, as it contains little or no pomegranate juice.

Makes about 1/2 cup

Date Honey

The righteous shall flourish like the palm tree...
those that be planted in the house of the Lord shall flourish...
they shall bring forth fruit in the old age;
they shall be fat and flourishing.

PSALMS 92:12–14

Dates *(Phoenix dactylifera)* are one of the world's oldest cultivated tree crops, yet, inexplicably, the fruit itself receives no mention in the Bible, even though palms are frequently cited. Biblical archaeologists have proven that date culture was well established in the Fertile Crescent as early as 3000 B.C. They also believe that, at one time, date palms virtually covered the entire Jordan River Valley. In Hebrew, the town of Bethany, the home of Martha, Lazarus, and Mary, two miles east of Jerusalem, literally means "house of dates." Date honey is one way in which biblical cooks made use of their abundant, sweet commodity. Use it as you would bee honey, or serve it as a dip for wedges of warm Unleavened Griddle Bread (see page 74) or Leavened Griddle Bread (see page 76). Or, blend the honey with equal parts of almond butter, pistachio butter, or sesame butter (tahini), to create an unusual spread for flatbread.

IN THE BEGINNING, THERE WAS HONEY

Refined sugar was unknown in biblical times. In its place, the people of the Holy Land used honey, honeycomb, or thick syrups or "honeys," made from grapes, pomegranates, or dates as condiments or dips for warm griddle bread. They also may have mixed the honey with nut and sesame butters to make delicious spreads.

¹/₂ pound pitted dates

3 cups boiling water

In a large bowl, combine the dates with 1 cup of the boiling water. Soak for 20 minutes.

Thoroughly mash the dates with your hands, squeezing them with your fingers. Add the remaining 2 cups of boiling water. Let stand for 5 minutes. Drain through a medium-mesh sieve set over a large bowl. Strain the pulp a second time through a fine-mesh sieve, pressing with the back of a wooden spoon to extract as much liquid as possible. Discard the pulp. Pour the liquid into a large nonreactive saucepan.

Cook over medium heat, stirring occasionally to prevent the mixture from sticking to the sides of the pan, until it has reduced to the consistency of molten honey, 40 to 45 minutes. Transfer to a glass jar with a tight-fitting lid and store in the refrigerator. The honey will keep for up to 3 months.

Note: You can purchase commercially made date honey, sometimes called *debbess,* in Middle Eastern markets.

Makes about 1¹/₂ cups

Homemade Red Wine

Drink no longer water, but use a little wine
for thy stomach's sake and thine often infirmities.

1 TIMOTHY 5:23

Paul's prescription for Timothy's recurring gastrointestinal problems may have been sound medical advice in an age far removed from water purification systems. Today, for different reasons, many physicians advocate modest consumption of red wine as part of a healthful diet.

The fermented "blood of the grape" was the most popular drink in biblical times. Winemakers extracted juice from their ripe fruit by trampling the grapes in rock-cut wine-presses. Wild yeasts occurred naturally on the grape skins, creating spontaneous fermentation in the crushed fruit (called "must"), thereby converting the grape sugar into alcohol and carbon dioxide. The latter by-product prompted the biblical admonition: "And no man putteth new wine into old bottles [wine skins]; else the new wine will burst the bottles, and be spilled, and the bottles shall perish" (Luke 5:37). Wild yeasts, however, produced wines of inconsistent quality.

Traditionally, the first wine of the season was taken to the temple, where it was given as an offering to God. Rich and poor alike consumed what remained. Drinking newly fermented wine was common practice. The lively quality of this incompletely fermented beverage, with its suspended yeast cells and tartrates (something akin to a very young, unfiltered *nouveau* Beaujolais) must certainly have been an acquired taste. Wine was also stored in "bottles" made from animal skins and aged in a cool place. Before it was served, it was always diluted with water, and was sometimes gently heated.

4 pounds red grapes (ripe, organi-
    cally grown wine grapes),
    unwashed (see Note), at room
    temperature

$^1/_{16}$ teaspoon (about 3 pinches)
    dry wine yeast (see Note)

1 teaspoon warm water

In a large bowl, mash and squeeze the grapes with your hands. Discard the larger stems. (Small stems, seeds, and grape skins add tannin, which help develop character and prolong the life of the wine.) Transfer the must to a half-gallon, glazed, earthenware crock. Dissolve the yeast in the water. Add to the must and stir. Cover and set aside at room temperature. Stir every 12 hours, for 5 to 6 days, or until the fermentation subsides (bubbling becomes negligible).

Strain through a large, fine-mesh sieve set over a bowl, using the back of a wooden spoon to extract as much wine as possible. Transfer to a clean 750 ml wine bottle, filling it to 1 inch above the top of the shoulder. (This limits the amount of air that can react with the wine and cause oxidation, affecting its taste.) Insert a clean cork into the bottle. Save extra wine in a small, clean bottle or jar (for topping off), and cover. Store both containers, undisturbed, in a cool, dark place for about 10 days, or until the suspended grape solids, yeasts, and tartrates (known collectively as lees or dregs) settle. Decant the wine to separate it from the lees. Pour into another clean 750 ml wine bottle and fill to 1 inch above the shoulder, using wine from the small bottle or jar. Insert a clean cork. Store horizontally, undisturbed, in a cool, dark place for about 4 months. Decant before serving.

Note: Try to use ripe, organically grown wine grapes. If they are not available, substitute red table grapes from your local market. Wash them carefully before using. Because table grapes are not picked at the peak of their ripeness, their sugar content will be less than that of wine grapes. To compensate for this, add $^1/_3$ cup bee honey or Grape Honey (see page 93). For a source of wine yeasts, see page 108. If you are able to find ripe, organically grown wine grapes, you may want to try using the wild yeast that occurs naturally on their skins to ferment the must.

Makes about 750 ml

New Wine
(or Fresh Grape Juice)

*And they came unto the brook of Eshcol, and cut down from thence
a branch with one cluster of grapes, and they bare it between two upon
a staff; and they brought of the pomegranates, and of the figs.*

NUMBERS 13:23

Grapes *(Vitus vinifera)* were the first cultivated plants mentioned in the Bible, and the most abundant fruit grown in the Holy Land. Wine is cited over 140 times in Scripture. In the biblical sense, the word "wine" simply meant the juice of the grape, fermented or unfermented. Like connoisseurs today, the ancient Hebrews preferred the former: "No man also having drunk old wine straightway desireth new…The old is better," states the parable in Luke 5:39. Nevertheless, after a long, hot day working in the fields, what biblical viticulturist could resist a bowl of sweet must from his freshly harvested grapes?

3 pounds seedless red or white grapes, at room temperature

In a large bowl, mash the grapes and squeeze them with your hands. Remove the large stems. Strain through a large, fine-mesh sieve set over a bowl, using the back of a wooden spoon to extract as much juice as possible. Discard the skins, seeds, and small stems. Serve chilled.

About 1 quart

TECHNIQUES

Cooking Lentils

Lentils do not need pre-soaking. Cover with water, stir, and discard any that float to the surface. Drain and transfer to a saucepan. Cover with 3 inches of water. Cook over moderate heat until they are tender, 20 to 25 minutes. Drain, reserving the cooking liquid for later use.

Grinding Lentils

It was not uncommon for biblical cooks to combine pulse meal with grain flour to make bread. You can purchase pulse meal (made from fava beans, garbanzo beans, or lentils) in Middle Eastern markets or health food stores. Pulse meal is also available through the mail; for sources, see page 109. You can also make your own pulse meal by grinding dried pulses in a grain mill or a spice grinder. Grinding $^1/_4$ cup whole pulses yields about $^1/_4$ meal.

Grinding Seeds

Grind seeds in an electric grinder or a stone grinding implement (like a Mexican *molcajete*). For toasted seeds, do not grind until they are completely cool.

Grinding Nuts

Grind nuts in an electric spice grinder, grain mill, or stone grinding implement (like a Mexican *molcajete*). For toasted nuts, do not grind until they are completely cool (or you may end up with nut butter).

Preparing Fava Beans

Fava beans are one of our most delicious inheritances from the ancients, but modern-day medicine has shown us that individuals deficient in Glucose-6-Phosphate Dehydrogenase (G6PD) sometimes suffer from an allergy to fava beans, known as favism. G6PD deficiency is the most common enzyme deficiency in humans. It can cause hemolytic anemia, the symptoms of which are pallor, headache, fatigue, jaundice, and shortness of breath following exertion. It affects close to 400 million people worldwide, many from the Mediterranean region, especially Greece.

Favas are available fresh and dried and, despite their reputation as labor-intensive beans, are easy to prepare.

FOR DRIED FAVA BEANS
Overnight method: Whole dried fava beans and fava bean halves are available in Middle Eastern markets. To prepare for use, place the dried beans in a bowl and cover them with water. Drain the beans and discard impurities. Cover with 3 inches of water. Soak for 12 to 24 hours. Drain again. At this point, you can remove the tough seed coats by placing the beans between two clean towels and rubbing them a few minutes, until the seed coats slip off.

To cook, transfer the beans to a heavy saucepan. Cover with 3 inches of water. Bring to a boil and skim off the foam. Reduce the heat to medium and cook, covered, until the beans are tender, 2 to 2$\frac{1}{2}$ hours. (The older the dried beans, the longer they will take to cook.) Drain, reserving the cooking liquid for later use.

Quick-soak method: Place the beans in a bowl and cover them with water. Drain the beans and discard impurities. Place the beans in a large saucepan, and cover them with 3 inches of water. Cover the pan with a lid, bring to a boil, and cook for 3 minutes. Remove from the heat and let stand, covered, for at least 1 hour. Drain again, reserving the cooking liquid for later use. Remove the tough seed coats by placing the beans between two clean towels and rubbing them for a few minutes, until the seed coats slip off.

FOR FRESH FAVA BEANS

Select slender, 3- to 4-inch-long pods. These hold the smallest, most tender beans. Shell the beans and discard the pods. It is not necessary to peel young beans. Peeling is only recommended for larger, more mature beans that have a tough seed coat. To peel the beans, make a small incision at the hilum (small bump where the seed attaches to the pod) using your thumbnail, and squeeze each bean between thumb and forefinger until it pops out of its seed coat.

Packages of frozen fava beans are available in Middle Eastern markets.

Seeding Pomegranates

With a sharp knife, remove the skin and pith from the stem and blossom ends of each pomegranate, being careful not to cut into the red seeds inside. Score the skins several times from blossom end to stem end. Fill a large bowl with water. Holding each fruit under water, break it into sections. Using your fingers, separate the seeds from the skin and white pith. The seeds will sink to the bottom of the bowl, while the skin and pith will float to the surface. Discard the skin and pith. Pour the water and seeds into a colander. Rinse, removing any remaining bits of skin and pith.

Toasting Nuts

Place nuts on an ungreased baking sheet and toast them in a 350° oven for 10 to 12 minutes, or until the nuts turn a toasted brown color and are aromatic. Remove them from the oven and let cool on the baking sheet.

Toasting Seeds

Place $1/2$ cup of the seeds in a skillet over medium heat. Toast, stirring frequently, until the seeds are golden, 3 to 5 minutes. To toast in the oven, preheat the oven to 250°. Spread the seeds on a baking sheet. Toast, stirring once or twice, until the seeds are golden, 15 to 20 minutes.

SOURCES FOR SPECIALTY INGREDIENTS

The Baker's Catalogue
King Arthur Flour
P.O. Box 876
Norwich, VT 05055
(800) 827-6836
High-quality yeast, flour, and other ingredients,
plus books and baking tools.

The Bean Bag
P.O. Box 221430
Sacramento, CA 95822
(800) 845-BEAN
Lentils and fava and garbanzo beans.

Beer Crafts
845 West San Marcos Boulevard
San Marcos, CA 92069
(800) 728-8827
Vinegar starter and wine-making supplies.

Doc's Cellar
855 Capitolio Road #2
San Luis Obispo, CA 94301
(805) 781-9974
Mother-of-vinegar starters and
wine-making equipment.

Fiddyment Farms
5000 Fiddyment Road
Roseville, CA 95678
(916) 771-0800
Pistachios and pistachio butter.

Fusano California Valley
Specialty Olive Oil Co.
784 Main Street, Suite E
Cambria, CA 93428
(800) 916-5483
Olives and olive oil.

The Grain Mill
Home Bakers and Cooks Catalog
2432 Mission Avenue
Carmichael, CA 95608
(800) 675-0954
Grains and spices.

Great Fermentations California
136 Bellam Boulevard
San Rafael, CA 94901
(888) 570-WINE or (800) 570-BEER
Vinegar starters and wine-making supplies.

SPECIALTY INGREDIENTS

Jewel Date Co.
48440 Prairie Drive
Palm Desert, CA 92260
(760) 398-3551
Organically grown dates and date products.

Kalustyan Orient Export Co.
123 Lexington Avenue
New York, NY 10016
(212) 685-3451
Fava beans, lentil meals, and spices.

M. and C.P. Farms
3986 Road NN
Orland, CA 95963
(916) 865-9810
Fresh olives available mid-September through December. Wide variety of cured olives available year-round.

Nunes Farms
P.O. Box 311
Newman, CA 95360
(209) 862-3033
(800) 255-1641
Bulk almonds and pistachios.

Oasis Date Gardens
59-111 Highway 111
P.O. Box 757
Thermal, CA 92274
(800) 827-8017 or (760) 399-5665
Medjool dates, date sugar, and date butter.

Petrou Foods, Inc.
7930 Arjohns Drive, Suite B
San Diego, CA 92121
(619) 271-9983 or (619) 458-1981
Olives, olive oil, and vinegar.

Sciabica's Olive Oil
700 Kiernan Avenue, Unit 8
Modesto, CA 95356
(800) 551-9612
Organic varietal olive oils and vinegar.

The Spice House
1941 Central Street
Evanston, IL 60201
(847) 328-3711
Spices.

Timeless Seeds
P.O. Box 1296
Conrad, MT 59425
(406) 278-5770
Lentils.

Sourdoughs International
P.O. Box 670
Cascade, ID 83611
(800) 888-9567
Sourdough starters from around the world, including Giza and Red Sea starters.

For more information, visit Kitty Morse's home page at **www.kittymorse.com**

BIBLIOGRAPHY

Anderson, Stanley F. and Raymond Hull. *The Art of Making Wine.* New York: NAL-Dutton, 1971.

Apicius. *Cookery and Dining in Imperial Rome.* Edited and translated by Joseph Dommers Vehling. New York: Dover, 1977.

Bodenheimer, F.S. "The Manna of Sinai." *The Biblical Archaeologist,* 10 (1947): 2–6.

Bottero, Jean. "The Cuisine of Ancient Mesopotamia." *The Biblical Archaeologist,* 48 (1985): 36–47.

Bromiley, Geoffrey, ed. *The International Standard Bible Encyclopedia,* rev. ed. Grand Rapids, MI: W.B. Eerdmans, 1979.

British and Foreign Bible Society. The Holy Bible (King James version). London: Oxford University Press, 1928.

Corbier, Mireille. "The Ambiguous Status of Meat in Ancient Rome." *Food and Foodways,* 3 (1989): 223–264.

Crim, Keith R., ed. *The Interpreter's Dictionary of the Bible.* New York: Abingdon Press, 1962.

De Moor, Janny. "Eating Out in the Ancient Near East." *Proceedings of the Oxford Symposium on Food and Cookery.* London: 1991, pp. 212–231.

Edelstein, Gershon and Gibson, Simon. "Ancient Jerusalem's Rural Food Basket." *Biblical Archaeology Review,* 4 (1982): 46–54.

Encyclopedia Judaica Jerusalem, The. MacMillan Co., 1971.

Feeley-Harnik, Gillian. *The Lord's Table: The Meaning of Food in Early Judaism and Christianity.* Washington: Smithsonian Institution Press, 1994.

Frenkley, Helen. "The Search for Roots: Israel's Biblical Landscape Reserve." *Biblical Archaeology Review,* 5 (1986): 37–43.

Hastings, James, ed. *A Dictionary of the Bible,* 5 vols., set. Peabody, MA: Hendrickson Pubs, Inc., 1988.

Hawtin, Lorna. *Fava Bean Cookbook.* The International Center for Research in the Dry Areas (ICARDA). Aleppo, Syria: 1981.

Herodotus. *The Histories.* New York: Penguin, 1972.

Hesse, Brian. "Animal Husbandry and Human Diet in the Ancient Near East." Excerpted from *Civilizations of the Ancient Near East.* Sasson, Jack M., editor in chief. Vol. 1, Charles Scribner's Sons, Macmillan Library Reference USA. New York: 1995, pp. 203–222.

Hestrin, Ruth and Zeev Yeivin. "Oil from the Presses of Tirat-Yehuda." *The Biblical Archaeologist,* 40 (1977): 29–31.

Keller, Werner. *The Bible as History.* New York: Bantam, 1983.

Kislev, Mordechai E. "Early Neolithic Horsebean from Yiftah'el, Israel." *Science,* 288 (1985): 319–320.

Kosikowski, Frank. *Cheese and Fermented Milk Foods,* 2nd ed. Ithaca, NY: Cornell University, 1982.

Kurmann, Jos. A., et. al. *Encyclopedia of Fermented Fresh Milk Products: An International Inventory of Fermented Milk, Cream, Buttermilk, Whey, and Related Products.* New York: Van Nostrand Reinhold, 1992.

Lawton, John. *Mesopotamian Menus.* Aramco World, vol. 39, No. 2 (1988): 4–9.

Limet, Henri. "The Cuisine of Ancient Sumer." *Biblical Archaeologist,* 50 (1987): 132–140.

Lockyer, Herbert Sr., ed. *Illustrated Dictionary of the Bible.* Nashville: Thomas Nelson, 1997.

McGee, Harold. *On Food and Cooking: The Science and Lore of the Kitchen.* New York: Macmillian, 1988.

Moldenke, Harold N. and Alma L. Moldenke. *Plants of the Bible.* New York: Dover, 1986.

Nesbitt, Mark. "Plants and People in Ancient Anatolia. *The Biblical Archaeologist,* March 1995, 58:2, pp. 68–81

Neufeld, Edward. "Hygiene Conditions in Ancient Israel." *The Biblical Archaeologist,* 34 (1971): 8 1971(2), pp. 50–55.

New American Bible. New York: Catholic Book Publishing Co., 1970.

Nun, Mendel. "Cast Your Net Upon the Waters: Fish and Fishermen in Jesus' Time." *Biblical Archaeology Review,* 19 (1993): 47–56.

Renfrew, Jane M. "Vegetables in the Ancient Near Eastern Diet." *Civilizations of the Ancient Near East.* Sasson, Jack M., editor in chief. Charles Scribner's Sons, Macmillan Library Reference USA, 1 (1995): 191–202.

Rodale Press editors. *Rodale's Illustrated Encyclopedia of Herbs.* Emmaus, PA: Rodale Press, 1987.

Scott, R.B. "Weights and Measures of the Bible." *The Biblical Archaeologist,* XXII (1959): 22–40.

Singer, F., ed. *The Jewish Encyclopedia.* New York: Gordon Press, 1976.

Soler, Jean. Translated by Elborg Forster. "The Semiotics of Food in the Bible." *Food and Drink in History, Selections from the Annales: Economies, Societies, Civilizations,* 28 (July-August 1973, pp. 943–55). Baltimore, MD: Johns Hopkins University Press, 1979.

Tannahill, Reay. *Food in History.* New York: Random House, 1995.

The New English Bible: New Testament. London/Cambridge, MA: Oxford University Press/Cambridge University Press, 1961.

Wood, Ed. *World Sourdoughs from Antiquity.* Berkeley, CA: Ten Speed Press, 1996.

Zimmerman, Sybil. "Housewares and Recipes from 2000 Years Ago." *Biblical Archaeology Review,* VII (1981): 55–58.

ACKNOWLEDGMENTS

For their encouragement, I want to express my gratitude to friends and colleagues Carole Bloom; Ann Carli; and Susan Carrigan; Oscar Chung, O.D., and his wife, Jan; Betz Collins; Judy Eberhardt; Jim and Froukje Frost; June Kubli, Ph.D.; Andrea Peterson; Mary Rose; and Rachel Sayre.

I would also like to thank Dick and Margo Baughman, managers of the Vista, California, farmers' market; Jack Bloom, Ph.D., associate professor of sociology at Indiana State University; Frederick Holmshaw, owner of San Diego Artisan Bakers, Escondido, California; art historian Marion de Koning, William Erskine of the International Center for Argricultural Research in the Dry Areas (ICARDA), Aleppo Syria; author and edible plant expert Stephen Facciola; J. Travis Hart and his wife, Nancy, of Hart Winery, Temecula, California; professor emeritus Issa Khalil, Ph.D.; newsletter editor Karen Paulus, Wisconsin Center for Dairy Research, University of Wisconsin-Madison; Charles Perry, food historian and staff writer for the *Los Angeles Times;* and herb growers Suilin and Whitney Robinson.

And finally, for their invaluable assistance, I want to give special thanks to Chaldean friends Suhama and Elia Mansour; to Richard Shlemmer, Ph.D. and his wife, JoAnne; to my tireless agent, Julie Castiglia; to illustrator Diana Reiss and photographer Susanne Kaspar; to Nancy Austin, whose beautiful design truly captures the feeling of the Holy Land; to Lorena Jones, my diligent and patient editor; and to Ten Speed Press publisher Kirsty Melville, who shared my vision from the beginning.

INDEX

RECIPE INDEX